POSITIVELY M. A. D.

MAKING A DIFFERENCE

IN YOUR
ORGANIZATIONS,
COMMUNITIES,
& THE WORLD

STORIES AND IDEAS
FROM 50 OF TODAY'S
LEADING EXPERTS

EDITED BY
BILL TREASURER,
AUTHOR OF *RIGHT RISK*

BK

BERRETT-KOEHLER PUBLISHERS, INC.
San Francisco

Berrett-Koehler Publishers, Inc.
235 Montgomery Street, Suite 650
San Francisco, CA 94104-2916
Tel: (415) 288-0260   Fax: (415) 362-2512   www.bkconnection.com

Ordering Information

Quantity sales. Special discounts are available on quantity purchases by corporations,
associations, and others. For details, contact the "Special Sales Department" at the
Berrett-Koehler address above.

Individual sales. Berrett-Koehler publications are available through most bookstores.
They can also be ordered direct from Berrett-Koehler: Tel: (800) 929-2929; Fax:
(802) 864-7626; www.bkconnection.com

Orders for college textbook/course adoption use. Please contact Berrett-Koehler:
Tel: (800) 929-2929; Fax: (802) 864-7626.

Orders by U.S. trade bookstores and wholesalers. Please contact Publishers Group West,
1700 Fourth Street, Berkeley, CA 94710. Tel: (510) 528-1444; Fax (510) 528-3444.

Berrett-Koehler and the BK logo are registered trademarks of Berrett-Koehler
Publishers, Inc.

Printed in the United States of America

Berrett-Koehler books are printed on long-lasting acid-free paper. When it is available,
we choose paper that has been manufactured by environmentally responsible processes. These may include using trees grown in sustainable forests, incorporating recycled
paper, minimizing chlorine in bleaching, or recycling the energy produced at the paper
mill.

Library of Congress Cataloging-in-Publication Data
    Positively M.A.D. : making a difference in your organizations, communities, and
the world / edited by
    Bill Treasurer
        p.   cm.
    Includes index.
    ISBN 1-57675-312-3
        1. Social action.   2. Community action.   3. Social change.
I. Title: Positively MAD.   II. Treasurer, Bill, 1962–
HN17.5P698   2004
303.4—dc22   2004052995

FIRST EDITION
09 08 07 06 05 04   10 9 8 7 6 5 4 3 2 1

Text design by Detta Penna

Dedicated to our readers
and the clients we serve.
Thank you for making such a
positive difference in our worlds.

Madly,
The B-K authors

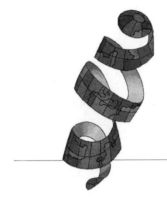

CONTENTS

CONTENTS

CONTENTS

CONTENTS

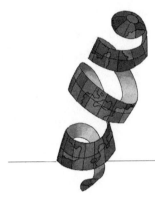

FOREWORD

by Geoff Bellman

This book is about people and organizations who are Positively Making A Difference. But before we get into their stories, I want to tell you a little about the extraordinary publisher who makes this book possible—and his publishing house whose self-defined purpose is "to create a world that works for all." Any business book about people making a difference should clearly begin with Berrett-Koehler.

In the late '80s, Steve Piersanti, Berrett-Koehler's founder, and I began talking. He was then president and CEO of Jossey-Bass Publishers. We were doing a book together *(The Consultant's Calling)* and I was lucky enough to have him as my editor, since most publishing house presidents do not edit books themselves. Steve's guidance through the editorial process gave me a lasting appreciation for the man who would create Berrett-Koehler Publishers a few years later.

In 1991, Steve received a career "nudge" from the Robert Maxwell publishing empire, the owners of Jossey-Bass: he was fired. Steve refused to lay off Jossey-Bass staff in order to meet Maxwell's demands to carry out a ten percent workforce reduction that Steve believed to be unwarranted and unjustified. Jossey-Bass was surpassing its sales and profitability goals—they needed more people, not fewer. Steve spoke truth to power and was terminated for sticking by his staff and his principles. I was among the many people who called Steve, commiserated, and asked what I could do to help. We agreed I would publish my next book with him. Then I called Peter Block and Marvin Weisbord and told them what had happened to Steve. They too moved to Berrett-Koehler and—along with Meg Wheatley—the four of us wrote early B-K best sellers, giving the company financial footing and a positive reputation in the marketplace. That's how this little company was founded—rooted in Steve's integrity and vision. I am proud to have participated in its creation.

More than thirteen years later, B-K continues to be a remarkable independent publisher. Steve and his people have been recognized with articles and awards, acknowledging their vision of contributing to the world, making it an enlightened place in which to live and work. B-K was started with Steve's non-corporate stance toward the world and the company lives that way today.

Three examples of how B-K does this . . .

First, by engaging its stakeholders—not just its stockholders: A few years ago, B-K held a Future Search conference. Authors, literary agents, publicists, consultants, business book readers, B-K book printers, copy editors, designers and artists, video producers, and staff were all invited to assist in creating the future of the company. Sixty-three people invested two days in imagining and planning what this innovative little publisher might become. How often do you see that happening in the corporate world?

Second, by getting to know B-K authors and their new books: Every book has an Author Day. The B-K staff gets to know the author, deepens their knowledge of the author as a person, while learning more about their new book. Together, staff and authors work out their roles in moving this book toward success. I've worked with four publishers; I've never been treated so well, personally and professionally, as I've been treated by Berrett-Koehler. Fellow B-K author David Korten says, "Berrett-Koehler [sets] a standard for integrity, professionalism, and author support without equal in the industry. Few experiences in my life have equaled the joy and sense of accomplishment that have come from the experience of working with the total support of such an exceptionally dedicated and talented editorial, design, and marketing team." You can hear the loyalty in David's words. Do you know how valuable that is?

And, you are already experiencing my third example: This *POSITIVELY M.A.D.* book flows from the B-K Authors Council, a gathering of authors that meets yearly, talks about books, and exchanges ideas about writing, publishing and marketing—and they pay their own way to do this! Since 1999, this Authors Council has become a committed community. This year, they decided to contribute to the world by writing this book and offering the "POSITIVELY M.A.D." conference held November 6, 2004. Do you know of many organizations that inspire this kind of willing contribution from stakeholders?

On my desk I have a quote attributed to Gandhi. "Whatever you do may seem insignificant, but it is most important that you do it." Berrett-Koehler is engaged in the hard work of publishing humane ideas for a corporate world that only occasionally seems to care. In staff meetings, planning retreats, and Author Days, B-K people remind themselves of their high values. They hold themselves to their self-defined standards. And, sometimes they wonder whether they are making a significant difference. They aspire to results which will not be realized in their own lifetimes — and perhaps not in the lifetime of this wonderful little company. And through it all, they know that whatever they are doing, it is most important that they do it.

○

Geoff Bellman is the author of three Berrett-Koehler books: *Getting Things Done When You Are Not in Charge (1992, 2001)*, *Your Signature Path (1996)*, and *The Beauty of the Beast (2000)*.

INTRODUCTION

There is an inverse relationship between initiative and enormity. The bigger and more challenging the issue, the less willing we are to face it head on. The trouble is, our world has "issues"—challenging, complex, and big . . . very big. There's the big stuff, like globalization, pollution, terrorism, jingoism, religious intolerance, and war. And the less big stuff, like offshore outsourcing, a broken healthcare system, an obesity epidemic, and rising gas prices. But it's all big stuff.

The challenges faced by our increasingly frenetic world are enough to make you throw up your hands in resignation. "Why bother?" you ask. "I can't make a difference anyway."

"*Au contraire,*" say we! And this book sets out to prove it.

Who are "we" you ask? First and foremost, we're authors. Authors with opinions and ideas that we're not afraid to share. Second, we're authors who have all published books with Berrett-Koehler Publishers. B-K tirelessly promotes ideas that elevate the human condition. Third, we're MAD. Really MAD. Steaming MAD in fact.

As authors, our expertise is varied. But the outcome we all aim for is strikingly similar—to leave the world better off than we found it. And our MADness allows us to do this.

In spiritual literature, there is a concept called *holy anger*. It is the notion that our dissatisfactions (sometimes referred to as "divine discontent") can be our fuel for making an enduring impact on the world. It is this holy anger, this dissatisfaction with the inadequacies of the present, that brings about the change necessary to create a better future. This is the idea behind *Positively M.A.D.*

Despite the complexity of the world's problems and inadequacies, and despite our own frustration with the current state of affairs, we *can* indeed **Make A D**ifference. Regardless of our station in life, each of us is entitled, if not obliged, to etch our initials onto the tree of humanity.

In the stories and descriptions that follow, you'll learn of people just like you who are making a true difference in the world. You'll learn about contemporary ideas from some of the world's leading thinkers. Though MAD, in some instances certifiably so, our MADness is directed at a purposeful aim: to help you take action in your own life in order to make a positive difference in the organizations and communities you serve. In the end, we think you will be inspired to make a difference in your world.

The chapters of *Positively M.A.D* are organized into twelve lessons (outlined below). Each lesson is composed of a number of stories that illustrate, with real-life examples, how to make a meaningful difference in the world. Each story contains a number of MAD Tips that can be immediately applied in your life. Sometimes these tips are included as part of the story, at other times the tips appear at the story's end.

12 Lessons For Being Positively M.A.D.:

1. **Embrace Your MADness:** The stories in this chapter underscore why it is important to move toward your madness. It is the people with an almost obsessive passion who get the most done. The toughest part is sticking to it when everyone around you is convinced that you're crazy.

2. **Have A Higher Purpose:** Making a difference takes energy and effort. This chapter describes how having a higher purpose helps you stay goal-focused, thus sustaining your motivation in the face of obstacles and setbacks.

3. **Find Common Ground:** Rarely can you, or should you, do it alone. Lasting impact often requires bringing together people who see the world in different ways. As this chapter illustrates, by focusing on their common purpose, rather than their points of friction, diverse people can come together to change the world.

4. **Lead Earnestly:** Often the impact of a single person extends far beyond normal expectations. This chapter shows how an enduring difference is often a by-product of a single person's influence earnestly applied.

5. **Mobilize Committed People:** It takes more than a long lever to move the world. It takes committed people directing their efforts toward a worthwhile aim. The stories in this chapter demonstrate that the best way to get things done is to *share the madness!*

6. **Capitalize on Adversity:** This chapter includes stories about people who have done more than just overcome adversity . . . they've actually capitalized on their adversity and leveraged it to their advantage.

7. **Defy Convention:** As the saying goes, *if you always do what you've always done, you'll always get what you've always gotten.* This chapter includes stories about people who refuse to stick to stale approaches and outdated responses. They rely on, and relish, unconventional approaches.

8. **Shift Perspective:** The stories in this chapter show how sometimes the only thing standing between you and the difference you can make is a slight shift in perspective.

9. **Work With City Hall:** MAD people, as this chapter illustrates, don't always buck the system. Rather, they bring about profound change by working within the system. Sometimes they even change the system by working the system itself.

10. **Stand Up to Authority:** Sometimes those with the power to make a difference, stand in the way of the difference being made. This chapter includes stories of MAD people who are self-assured enough to stand up, and *speak up,* to authority.

11. **Pay Attention to the Little Things:** As the stories in this chapter show, the best way to make a difference in the world isn't with grandiose plans. Sometimes it's the little ordinary things, consistently and persistently applied, that bring about the most profound changes.

12. **Express Gratitude:** People who are truly MAD aren't doing it alone. As related in this chapter, they benefit from the good works of many people. As such, people who are MAD take the risk of being vulnerable by expressing sincere gratitude. In so doing, they improve morale, deepen relationships, and give others a reason to work hard.

EMBRACE YOUR MADNESS

First Among Equals
by Don Frick

By 1991, George SanFacon was weary of mediocrity and isolation in the workplace. He had worked as a cook, mechanic, custodian, engineer, trainer, teacher, painter, and consultant. Everywhere, he saw a lack of community and few efforts to meet human needs. "Mediocrity not only sabotaged the desired outcomes of organizations," says George, "but created a killing field of the human spirit."

Now he was director of Housing Facilities at the University of Michigan in Ann Arbor, a department with several hundred employees, and he felt even more isolated. His people did their jobs well but were reluctant to connect, be authentic, and admit to faults. During a three-day silent retreat, George realized that his traditional management role of holding power over others created a climate of fear.

"Then I asked myself what love would look like in the workplace," remembers George. "What would I do if my mother reported to me, or my sons? I knew that I would want them to be true partners with me in the enterprise. That's what love would look like. Then I realized that the people reporting to me *were* mothers and sons from other families. And so I decided to change the framework." It was time to step out and live the change he sought to create, even though he did not yet know what form it would take.

George went to his management team and said, "We have high burnout and low morale and I'm part of the problem. I'm asking you to find an outside person to help us go forward." They contacted a facilitator who led a retreat where managers could vent their frustrations with George—and with each other—in a "safe container." The trust-building process had begun.

About the same time, George discovered in Robert Greenleaf's essay "The Institution as Servant," the conceptual model he had been seeking—a structure where the designated leader operates as a "first among equals" in building consensus. George decided to give up unilateral control for a system of shared governance, thereby becoming a peer-level decision maker on a council of equals with his top managers. No one was forced to participate in this experiment but they all did.

By 2004 the organizational chart looked like a mandala, with "an integrated network of overlapping teams that lead and manage the enterprise, enabling the department to achieve significantly higher levels of performance" according to the *Facilities Council Handbook*. Every council member formally signs a charter pledging to work within the framework in good faith and to the best of their abilities. The university has approved the charter.

Today, no one person alone can hire, fire, promote, or evaluate an employee. It is done by group process and consensus. By the time of George's retirement in the spring of 2004, the commitment to a consensus structure was embedded in the hearts and minds of many partners. George reminds us that "Creating better workplaces is not different than creating better selves and a better world."

M.A.D TIPS *By George SanFacon

- Be willing to look at yourself first and your need for power. We are all broken but are more than our brokenness. This model won't work unless you come from a deep place.
- You don't have to know the answers; you only need to steward a process of dialogue and consensus decision making. People will support what they help to create.
- Go for the long haul. This work takes time.

○

For more information on the Housing Facilities governance structure, visit the University of Michigan website (www.housing.umich.edu/pdfs/FacHandbook.pdf) where you can download the council handbook and George SanFacon's book *Awake at Work: Concepts and Principles for Creating Better Workplaces and a Better World.*

Don M. Frick is author of *Robert K. Greenleaf: A Life of Servant Leadership.*

Creative Convincing for Corporate Change

by Pamela Gordon

Ian's ultimate goal was for his corporation to waste zero resources: "At the end of each day, I want only people and finished product to leave the plant."

"Impossible," you say? What "impossible" goals do *you* have for organizational change? And if you don't have any, then why not? You have full permission to envision and foster healthier organizations—for people, profit, and/or planet. See how Ian is well on his way to meeting his goal—leveraging his passion, know-how, and creative convincing of others.

Ian McKeown loves his area of the world—the Leven Valley near Glasgow, Scotland. With its bonny Loch Lomond, rolling green hills, and a meandering river, you would too. The Leven River draws a half-circle around Polaroid's manufacturing plant, where Ian is the environmental manager. When Ian talks to Polaroid's managers about adopting procedures that will save money for the company and reduce waste, he uses his training and experience, love of the Leven Valley, and persistence.

At first Ian received many "no's" to his ideas about manufacturing, packaging, and shipping goods differently to reduce expensive waste. One of his most effective techniques is to repeatedly ask seemingly innocent questions about current procedures, until he overcomes people's resistance to trying new processes that will benefit the environment. Ian espouses the Japanese practice Ask Why Five Times. He finds that although people may first respond defensively when asked why or why not, gradually they lose their defensiveness and become open to the idea.

My favorite of Ian's creative convincing techniques is the one he used to persuade the film division's management and operators to use recycling bins. The operators, after testing the quality of the film, used to drop the scrap—film, plastic, and metal parts—into the trash. Management at first rejected Ian's idea for separating and recycling the scraps, claiming that the operators would not want to do so. Knowing that there was a dispute at the time between management and the operators, Ian said to the operators, "Management told me that you wouldn't want to use the bins." That clinched it—the operators agreed to use the recycling bins (in part, perhaps, to spite management).

Ian told me, "You use what you can and most of the time it's easy, as people do want to do a good job." Thanks to people like Ian McKeown, whose waste-reduction ideas have saved his corporation millions of dollars each quarter, a good job for the planet is usually a good job for profit.

If I asked *you* Five Times, would you latch onto *your* "impossible" corporate goals, and drive to "yes" with all your passion, know-how, and creative convincing?

- Notice corporate waste—whether environmental or otherwise—and give yourself permission to feel disgusted by it.

9

- Use that emotional energy to create ideas for improving the health of the organization, its customers and shareholders, the community, and the environment.
- Gain endorsement for your ideas using business language: lead your points with profit in mind—starting with the strategies that yield the highest rewards to profit and planet.

○

Pamela J. Gordon, Certified Management Consultant, is author of *Lean and Green: Profit for Your Workplace and the Environment (Berrett-Koehler, 2001),* and president of Technology Forecasters, Inc.—Helping technology executives reduce manufacturing costs and meet environmental goals profitably: www.techforecasters.com.

Be Who You Are
by Mark Levy

How can you make a difference in your organization and in the world? I know of a small yet potent way: Make sure your job reflects who you really are, because who you really are is where your energy lies. Let me illustrate what I mean by telling you about Joel Bauer.

Bauer is a trade show pitchman who *The Wall Street Journal Online* calls "the chairman of the board" of corporate trade show rainmaking. Over the course of his career, Bauer estimates that he's pitched to twenty million people, and has created three million leads for his clients.

What's his secret? He understands human nature. Bauer knows that what fascinates him will fascinate others—and he brings that knowledge to his work.

Since he was six years old, Bauer has been addicted to unusual entertainment forms, such as magic, stage hypnosis, and carnival stunts. At a trade show, then, he uses a number of intriguing entertainment tools to capture and sway a crowd.

For instance, he might charge into an aisle, cock a rubber band in one hand, and fire it along the floor, where the band rolls forty feet, fast, fast, fast, and just as everyone thinks it's about to die, it reverses direction and races back to his waiting hand.

Or, he'll read the mind of a volunteer who he's never met before.

Or, he'll use his fingertips to divine the serial number on a borrowed dollar bill, while his eyes are sealed with gauze pads and electrical tape.

Whatever the oddity, you can be sure that it's helped him attract a crowd, and once that crowd is happy, Bauer starts his pitch.

To be more effective, try approaching your work like Bauer approaches his. That doesn't mean you should shoot rubber bands and read minds. What it means is that you needn't wall up who you really are when you get to work.

- *Think about making a hobby part of your business.* I know a man who wanted to give seminars on financial planning, but thought numbers would bore his audience. How did he overcome this hurdle? Besides being a planner, he was also a jazz guitarist, so instead of dry seminars, he gave "financial concerts." He'd play the guitar, discuss finance, and use one subject to shed light on the other.

- *Think about making a much-loved past career part of your current career.* Bill Treasurer, the man who compiled this book, did just that. For ten years, he excelled as a professional theme-park daredevil. Bill's act? He'd climb a ten-story tower, set himself on fire, and dive into a water tank. Eventually, he wanted a new challenge, so he went into coaching and consulting—and took his daredevil ethic with him. Now, Bill's company, Giant Leap Consulting, builds courage in organizations by teaching leaders and employees how to take important business risks.

○

Mark Levy is the founder of Levy Innovation, a marketing strategy firm that makes people and companies compelling. He is the author, or co-creator, of four books, including *Accidental Genius: Revolutionize Your Thinking Through Private Writing (Berrett-Koehler, 2000),* which has been translated into five languages. Visit him on the web at www.levyinnovation.com.

Wayne's World
by Bill Treasurer

Wayne Bland sounds apologetic as he recounts the story, fully aware of its absurdity. He cites his failed suicide attempt as the reason he's able to make such a positive impact on people today.

"Listen," he says, "I'm telling you from experience that it is precisely when things seem most helpless, when your crisis is most intense, that your breakthrough is ready to occur."

Crisis had grabbed Wayne, at the age of 42, by the throat. Life had gotten bleak and hollow. His twin girls had left for college, his marriage had soured, and he had just quit his job. For Wayne, the afterlife was preferable to midlife.

"I had heard that drowning in cold water was a relatively peaceful death. So, on this dreary November day, I drove to the inlet, walked down to where the channel current was the strongest, and got ready to let the outgoing tide sweep me out to sea."

At the time, Wayne felt like the world was a bitter place. A place where no one could be trusted, especially the people Wayne called the "Leader Liars"—the rulers of the government, big corporations, and the church. Looking back, though, Wayne thinks his suicidal rage had less to do with his disappointment with the rulers of the world, and more to do with his disappointment with himself. He hated the fact that, despite endless opportunities, he hadn't done a single thing to improve the world. All he had done

EMBRACE YOUR MADNESS

was point a finger at it. "Ultimately," he says, "suicide isn't about anger. It's about selfishness."

So there he was, steeped in self-pity, ready to end it all. And then something unusual happened. Something . . . well . . . mad. There by the water's edge, a dolphin popped up his head, squawked loudly, and swam back under. Wayne, startled, wiped his eyes. Just as he regained his focus, he could see *two* dolphins squawking away at him. "This may sound crazy," he says, "but I believe they were God's messengers trying to talk me out of it. Two ocean angels."

Today Wayne Bland is known as "The Recovery Baron." He is the founder of Recovery Place, Inc. in Savannah, Georgia, which has treated over 7000 people for drug and alcohol abuse. Ironically, Wayne now devotes his life to touching the lives of people who, like he once did, have seemingly lost all hope.

Asked what he learned from his crisis moment nearly 20 years ago, Wayne is reflective. "Look, it's just plain more productive to walk through your crisis moment than to run from it. It's when you hit rock bottom that there's no place to go but up. So when madness pays you a visit, use it. I drew up the plans for Recovery Place *the same day* that the ocean angels saved my life."

Do you want to make a difference in the world? It might help to start by exploring the things you've learned in your moments of crisis. Sometimes what looks like insanity, or even madness, may be the entry point for valuable lessons that can be used to touch the lives of others. This is what it means to be a wounded healer. Taking your pain and putting it to good use.

M.A.D TIPS

- When your life takes a mad turn for the worse, hang on to the knowledge that *it's always darkest before the dawn.*
- During times of madness, ask yourself, "How can I embrace this craziness instead of run from it? How can I put it to good use?"
- Remember, there is no coming into consciousness without pain. What seems at first like madness, may in fact be your awakening into a more sober and more reality-based life.

O

Bill Treasurer loves being in the midst of people's courage. He is founder of Giant Leap Consulting, a courage-building company, and the author of *Right Risk: Ten Powerful Principles For Taking Giant Leaps With Your Life (Berrett-Koehler, 2003)*. He also served as the editor of this book. To learn more about Giant Leap Consulting, go to www.giantleapconsulting.com. To learn more about Recovery Place, call (912) 355-1440.

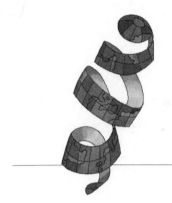

HAVE A HIGHER PURPOSE

The Antidote To Employee Apathy
by Paul Levesque

A visit to the home of Mr. Potato Head illustrates how some companies imbue their employees with a "sense of higher purpose" that makes their work feel far more meaningful and satisfying—while also making a positive difference in the world at large.

Rhode Island-based Hasbro Inc. is one of the nation's largest manufacturers and marketers of games and toys—and one of the most public-spirited corporations in the world. In 2004, the company was presented with the annual Excellence in Corporate Philanthropy award by actor Paul Newman (cofounder of The Committee to Encourage Corporate Philanthropy).

The Hasbro Charitable Trust was established in 1983. In 1994, the doors of the Hasbro Children's Hospital—a state-of-the-art pediatric and family care facility—opened in Providence, Rhode Island. In 1999 the company launched the Team Hasbro employee volunteer program, which qualifies most full-time employees for four hours of paid time off each month to volunteer for a child-focused charity. America's first corporate Boundless Playground (outfitted with special equipment that allows children in wheelchairs to play with others who are not similarly encumbered) was built by Hasbro employees. Wayne Charness, the executive responsible for corporate communications (including the Charitable Trust), estimates there are now 100-plus such playgrounds across the country, with more on the way.

In 2003, to mark the twentieth anniversary of its Charitable Trust, Hasbro made a special presentation to all its employees, which included a video segment in which World Vision president Rich Stearns documented the effects of Hasbro's philanthropy on children around the world. When guest speaker Sister Emerita McGann from Kentucky extended an impassioned *thank you* for the joy Hasbro's corporate generosity has brought to children in her care, children living in the midst of the most stifling poverty in America, "there wasn't a dry eye in the house," Charness acknowledges. When one observes employees identifying with their organization's objectives with such depth of feeling—in vivid contrast to so many business presentations where employees are visibly disinterested and openly cynical—one inevitably feels the urge to ask, is this not the way working for a living is supposed to feel? Is this not *important*?

Students of human motivation such as Abraham Maslow describe a hierarchy of human needs: once basic survival issues have been addressed, other needs come into play, such as a need for self-worth, a need to feel "useful and necessary in the world."

This means that for most workers a regular paycheck, while essential for survival, will never be enough in and of itself to generate higher meaning in their work. "You want to work hard for *something*," Charness says. Philanthropic companies like his give their employees precisely that "something"—a sense that the work they do for a living is making a positive difference in the world.

Even in less philanthropic companies, employees can still find ways to make a difference in their work. Simply choosing to be especially courteous and caring to customers, or especially helpful to co-workers, can become a personal form of giving— philanthropy on a one-on-one basis—and it can generate the same kind of personal satisfaction and sense of accomplishment.

As Wayne Charness puts it, "People like the combination of doing good and doing well at the same time."

- Choose a worthy cause for your own organization to get behind, one that most employees can relate to and will therefore be more inclined to support.
- If possible, choose a worthy cause that in some way links to the organization's basic business.
- Create opportunities for employees to become *volunteers* and get personally involved in the worthy cause.

○

Paul Levesque is co-author (with Art McNeil) of *Dreamcrafting: The Art of Dreaming Big, The Science of Making It Happen* (Berrett-Koehler, 2003). More on his study of philanthropy as an employee motivator can be found in his forthcoming book *Flashpoint!*

When the Path Takes a Turn (or Two)
by Jesse Stoner

She was the first female executive in the 150-year history of the large manufacturing company, The Stanley Works, maker of Stanley tools. Tall, slender, with short blonde hair, her direct, yet easygoing style allowed her to fit well with Stanley's male-dominated culture. Reporting directly to the CEO, Barbara Bennett had accomplished what few other corporate women had—she had broken through the glass ceiling.

At that time, she was my client and I worked closely with her in a variety of ways to align Stanley's culture and business strategies. She was absolutely committed to making a difference, for the company and the individuals within it. Convinced that breaking down barriers was in the best interest of the company, she was exceptionally creative in finding ways to do so. For example, years before either of us had heard about "large group interventions," Barbara asked me to help her plan a "working meeting" for their annual managers' meeting, where they would make real business decisions. I had never done anything like that before but thought it was a great idea. The meeting was a smashing success and took down many psychological walls. We appreciated and enjoyed each other, and over time, we became real friends.

About eight years ago her boss retired, and the new CEO had plans to remake the culture. At odds with where the company was going, Barbara decided to take an early retirement. I was concerned about what my dear friend would do without a job to keep her focused and without a corporate identity to hang her hat on. She was only in her mid-fifties—far too young to retire.

Boy was I wrong! Barbara entered the next phase of her life with the same enthusiasm that drove her to the top. Only this time, she focused on her own personal development. No more fancy titles. No ego involvement. I watched in amazement as her crisp business edge softened. She began meditating, studying healing and spirituality, and volunteering regularly at a hospice.

A couple of years ago Barbara announced that she was going to clown school. Once again, I wondered what she was up to. She sent me a "graduation" picture. Absolutely adorable. But why be a clown? I don't think she knew at first. As she put it, she just had a strong desire to learn to be a clown. But once again, she wove the strands of her life into a fabric that makes sense. She began to visit nursing homes and hospitals as a clown. In "clown face," Barbara was amazed that people would open up to her immediately and start talking about their deepest hopes and fears in ways they never would with an ordinary volunteer. Clowns break down barriers!

Has Barbara really changed? She has always wanted to break down barriers and make a difference. Where once she was a role model for many women and someone who had a huge sphere of influence, she now has a different kind of power. She uses the power, not to change people, but to help them discover joy and to be present with them in whatever place they are. To me this is the most powerful way to make a difference—touching people deeply.

Barbara's path has taken some unexpected turns. At times she hasn't been clear where the path was leading. However, she continues to focus on her purpose and trust herself to know that she doesn't have to have it all figured out—eventually the connection will be revealed.

- If you are clear about your purpose, trust yourself and trust the process, even though, at times, you don't know where it is taking you.
- Think big, act small. The person in front of you is your "client," no matter who that person is. Focus on him or her, while keeping in mind what is in the best interest of the larger organization.
- Visit www.seapointcenter.com or read *Full Steam Ahead! Unleash the Power of Vision* to learn more about how to create a compelling vision that will provide focus, energy, and direction and will guide you over the long term.

○

Jesse Stoner, co-author of the business best seller *Full Steam Ahead! Unleash the Power of Vision in Your Company and in Your Life*, is a partner in Seapoint

HAVE A HIGHER PURPOSE

Center, which helps people in organizations create a shared vision and the strategies to achieve it (www.seapointcenter.com).

Renewing Passion Through the Legacy of Contribution
by Chip R. Bell

Apathy comes in many forms. It can be complete emotional indifference, the sleep-walking movement of a factory worker, or the wooden sound in the operator's voice. Apathy robs teams of energy, marriages of romance, and organizations of much needed productivity. It is not a life-threatening malady—no one ever died from apathy—it is simply a spirit-killing one.

We live in an era of passion larceny. Downsizing has robbed colleagues of colleagues, leaving them hollow. Constant reorganizing has not only reshuffled key alliances, it has stolen valued allegiances. And, the heartless hustle for razor-thin margins has too often put short-term profits at center stage and long-term partnerships in the cheap seats. As the soul of the organization is put in a profit-at-all-cost vise, what is squeezed out is the positive spirit of workers.

How do leaders turn lethargy into energy? Some leaders point to the appeal of a compelling vision. Some rely on the WIIFM (What's In It For Me) of great economic returns. CEO Brad Schreier inspires employees to focus on their legacy by helping them remember the past.

"How would you like people to remember the contribution you made while you were here?" Schreier asks his associates at Taylor Companies Corporation headquarters in Mankato, MN. His message continues with thoughts like: Assume your children are not just inheriting your stuff but also the sounds of people talking about the work you did here. Would that message be one that would make you proud? If not, then start making it one today.

Great leaders know that as people remember the past they could leave behind, they passionately pursue the future they can create ahead. Helping people see how they contribute to the future is a vital part of the role of a great leader. Helping them discover how they contribute to a rich history is also a part of that role.

At a turning point in Taylor's history, Brad Schreier elected to address every manager from the eighty-five companies throughout North America, Europe and Australia that make up the privately-held corporation. One attendee recalled his message this way: "He reminded us that we were all standing on the shoulders of the pioneering giants who came before us. But we are the people on whose shoulders others will stand in the future. It is the quality of our work that insures they have a sound footing."

Passion comes from the kind of belief in the future that gives us security. It also emerges from a legacy of the past that arms us with substance. Great leaders don't let employees forget their corporate ancestry. Not to perpetuate an ineffective "we've always done it that way," but rather to honor the emotional ground on which the organization stands.

M.A.D
TIPS

- Use the organization's history as a way to build pride and inspire the building of something even grander.
- Let employees know they will be judged, not by who they knew or what they knew, but by what they left behind.
- Help employees craft a "Last Will and Testament" outlining what their organization will inherit when they depart.

○

Chip R. Bell is a renowned keynote speaker and Dallas-based consultant on customer loyalty. He is the author or co-author of several best-selling books, including three published by Berrett-Koehler—*Customers As Partners (1994), Managers As Mentors (2002)* and his newest book *Magnetic Service: Secrets for Creating Passionately Devoted Customers (2003).* He can be reached through www.chipbell.com.

And If You Had That, What Would You Have?

by David Schmaltz

Clients always try to undermine consultants. They do this innocently by focusing upon measurable goals. We too easily neutralize real improvement with unspoken conditions, degrading work into derivative, number-driven effort when it could have been purposeful pursuit. Making a real difference might require co-opting these innocent incapacitations.

When a large New York financial institution contracted with us to deliver project management workshops, the agreement focused on the usual terms and conditions: schedule, content, target audience, and cost. The need was obvious.

Accepting a hefty retainer, we interviewed staff, confident in our ability to provide a solution. We heard about all the usual difficulties, but something seemed to be missing from these conversations. Who sponsors workshops for the purpose of sponsoring workshops? Even acknowledging the company's aspirations, improving project performance seemed like a hollow target. We realized that we had bought into a purposeless effort, another one just like the projects we were supposed to help the client improve.

We scheduled time with the executive sponsor to make the distinction between goal and purpose. After several rounds of "And if you had that, what would you have?" he sighed deeply and began, "Several years ago, I was stationed in Germany working with Air Force intelligence. The Berlin Wall was coming down and the security challenges were overwhelming. We were several months into incredibly stressful, forced overtime, when one of my young sergeants had a paralyzing stroke. We sent him home on a stretcher." He paused before continuing. "I see some of the same patterns here, and I've invited you here to help my staff learn how to better cope with the stress, so I won't have to repeat that sorry meeting I had with my sergeant's wife."

Whew! My partner and I brushed away tears as we

acknowledged that we had just heard a real purpose. "Have you told anyone else this story?" we asked.

"No," he replied. "I still feel guilty about that situation."

We continued interviewing staff the next day, repeating the executive's story with each conversation. A remarkable resonance emerged. Everyone could relate to the story, and each found within it compelling reasons to do more than simply comply with his directive to attend the class.

Project performance improved. Clear purpose made the real difference.

Managers: The next time you assign an objective, articulate a juicy purpose for engaging. It's not achieving the goal but the juiciness of the purpose behind it that makes every pursuit worthwhile.

Consultants: Before accepting a juicy retainer to pursue some numbing objective, ask uncomfortable questions until some juicy purpose emerges. Asking "And if you had that, what would you have?" five times should help uncover a juicy enough purpose to justify even the largest retainer.

We can numb each other with our numbers and lose our purpose in our means for finely measuring success. When you cannot uncover this juiciness wherein the clients can expose their vulnerability, you might be best advised to simply send back the retainer and move on to where you can really make a difference. How could any result fully satisfy an unacknowledged purpose?

- What responsibilities are numbing you today? Noticing where the energy isn't will tell you where it might belong.
- Continue asking, "And if you had that, what would you have?" until the juiciness appears. The quality of the target always influences the quality of the pursuit.

○

David A. Schmaltz is the author of *The Blind Men and the Elephant,* and *Mastering Project Work (Berrett-Koehler, 2003),* and founder of True North pgs, a strategic Brief Consultancy™. "In the instant between perception and action, belief and behavior, lies the power to change the world." (www.projectcommunity.com)

Naming Our Life's Calling
by Richard Leider and David Shapiro

A few years ago, on a business trip to Boston, a cabbie reminded me of how naming our life's calling can make all the difference.

"So, whattayou in town for?" he asked me as we pulled away from the airport.

"I'm giving a presentation to some business people," I said, hoping to make it sound uninteresting so the driver would leave me alone.

He didn't take the hint. "Oh yeah? What's it about?"

I wasn't interested in giving the speech twice, so I offered the Reader's Digest abridged version. "Hearing and heeding your life's calling. Doing the work you were born to do."

My cabbie scoffed. "Your life's 'calling?' C'mon, I drive a cab here. What's that got to do with a calling?"

I closed my folder and caught the driver's eyes in the rearview. "You weren't born to drive a taxi?"

He just laughed.

"But you like your work well enough?"

He shrugged. "I guess it has its moments."

"I'm interested. What are those moments?"

"You mean besides quittin' time?"

I leaned forward and put my hand on the front seat. "I'm serious. Is there any time you feel like you're really bringing all of yourself to what you do?"

He smirked like he was going to say something sarcastic but then stopped. Gradually, his face softened. He laughed a little and said, "Well, there's this old lady."

I stayed silent and he continued.

"A couple times a week, I get a call to pick her up and take her to the grocery store. She just buys a few items. I help her carry them into her apartment, maybe unload them for her in her kitchen, sometimes she asks me to stay for a cup of coffee. It's no big deal, really; I'm not even sure she knows my name. But I'm her guy. Whenever she calls for a taxi, I'm the guy that goes. And I dunno, just makes me feel good. I like to help out."

"There's your calling right there," I said.

"What?" The smirk returned. "Unloading groceries?"

"You said you like to help out. That's a pretty clear expression of calling."

A smile spread across his face. "Well, I'll be damned. I guess that's right. Most of the time, I'm just a driver, but when I get that chance to help somebody—as long as they're not some kinda jerk or something—that's when I feel good about this job. So, whattayou know? I got a calling."

He fell silent for the rest of the trip. But I could see his face in the rear-view mirror and even when we hit the midtown traffic, he was still smiling.

That smile stays with me today and reminds me of an essential truth: the more of ourselves we bring to what we do and the more clearly we articulate that—by naming our life's calling in simple, straightforward terms—the more likely we are to find satisfaction and fulfillment in all that we do.

- Ask yourself, "When do I bring all of me to what I do?"
- Name your calling in simple straightforward terms.
- Make a difference by living your calling.

○

Richard J. Leider is a founding partner of the Inventure Group, a coaching and consulting firm in Minneapolis, MN, devoted to bringing out the natural potential in people. Author and co-author of six books, including the best seller *Repacking Your Bags: Lighten Your Load for the Rest of Your Life (Second edition,*

HAVE A HIGHER PURPOSE

Berrett-Koehler, 2002) and *Claiming Your Place at the Fire: Living the Second Half of Your Life on Purpose (Berrett-Koehler, 2004),* Richard is also an online columnist for *Fast Company.*

David A. Shapiro is a writer, philosopher, and educator who finds himself drawn again and again—both personally and professionally—to questions about the meaning and purpose of our lives. David is the author of *Choosing the Right Thing to Do: In Life, at Work, in Relationships, and For the Planet (Berrett-Koehler, 1999),* and is co-author with Richard J. Leider of three books, including their newest, *Claiming Your Place at the Fire: Living the Second Half of Your Life on Purpose (Berrett-Koehler, 2004).*

Our Only Choice Is to Make It Work
by Robert Jacobs

Have you ever been so tired of trying to make a difference that you felt like giving up? The odds were too long. Others had already tried and come up short.

That's what Nata Preis and her staff tackle five days a week. Nata is the principal at Village Glen School for children with special needs in Culver City, California.

"By the time we see these children, their self-esteem has been beaten back so much it's miniscule. We start by helping them feel good about themselves and their peers. We celebrate what a student knows, not what they don't know. We help them not feel frightened if they fail. You can't learn if you're afraid to fail. Every human being needs to feel successful. Success builds confidence. Confidence leads to learning. Learning how to create your life empowers you to want to have a life. If these kids give up at such an early age, they never become active participants in their lives."

I know Nata Preis makes a difference. She and her staff have already made a difference in my life. My son Aaron is a bright, kind, articulate boy. But he had attended four schools in the past seven years, having trouble at each one. We could not tell what the problem was. His teachers said that Aaron would talk out of turn. He needed more of their attention than the other children. Each school had given up on him.

We took him to many experts. Each added their own diagnosis to describe his troubles. Our loving, kind-hearted son had become a list of medical acronyms. With courage and grace he made his way through each day the best he could.

Recently we discovered Aaron has Asperger's, a high functioning form of autism. For autistic children basic social cues are a mystery. Seeing others laugh, smile, furrow their brows, and create personal space are all reminders that they are living in a foreign land. Children on the autism spectrum can't readily understand other people's feelings. Nor are they able to articulate their own feelings all the time. Nata offers an analogy, "Imagine how frightening it would be for us to be forced to live in a culture we don't understand. Every day. All the time. That's the world these children live in. That's the fear they have woken up to and had to face for years in getting ready for school in the morning.

"Lots of people have given up on these kids. The difference

HAVE A HIGHER PURPOSE

we make is that we never do give up. We just have never said, 'There's nothing we can do.' Our only choice is to make it work."

- What can we learn from Nata? When you have no choice but to make it work, miracles happen on a regular basis.
- If you never give up, you find a way to make a positive contribution.
- When you assume there is something you can do that will make a difference, you find there is. Where others have given up, you succeed . . . Just ask Nata Preis.

○

Robert W. "Jake" Jacobs is founder and president of Robert W. Jacobs Consulting, a firm specializing in accelerated, sustainable change. He is the author/contributor to four books including Berrett-Koehler's *RealTime Strategic Change (1997)* and *You Don't Have to Do It Alone: How to Involve Others to Get Things Done (2004)*. You can visit Jake on the web at www.rwjacobs.com.

Aaron Feuerstein: A Beacon for Change

by Robert D. Marx, Karen P. Manz, and Charles C. Manz

On Aaron Feuerstein's seventieth birthday celebration, a conflagration threatened to destroy what it took three generations of his family to create. A fire enveloped one building after another of this CEO's Malden Mills in the early hours of December 12, 1995. It was described as the worst industrial fire ever in Massachusetts. Thirty-three workers were injured, thirteen severely, and most of the buildings were rendered useless. One thousand of the 2800 employees were left without a workplace.

If Malden Mills followed the example of other textile mills in New England, its owners would collect the insurance money and relocate to cheaper labor and land in the South or offshore. Malden's hapless employees would be left unemployed. With 3000 jobs lost, the towns of Lawrence and Methuen, Massachusetts would face a grim future.

"There will be a Malden Mills tomorrow," Feuerstein vowed in the darkest hour of the fire's devastation. Against all odds Finishing Building 2 was left standing and several new machines used to make the firm's famous Polartec™ product survived because they were still packed in trailers away from the fire.

Feuerstein, a devout Jew, decided to keep his hundreds of affected employees on payroll with health benefits. His employees vowed to "pay (him) back tenfold." Six weeks after the fire

HAVE A HIGHER PURPOSE

Polartec production was running 50 percent above pre-fire productivity and Feuerstein was proclaimed a national hero.

Almost two years later, with $300 million of insurance money and another $100 million borrowed, a new state-of-the-art factory opened where the ashes of the old mill once prevailed. However, amid the widespread acclaim for Feuerstein's courageous and compassionate leadership, dark clouds were gathering. The insurance settlement proved inadequate for rebuilding the factory and a declining economy and cheap knockoffs of Polartec fabric forced an honorable man to file for Chapter 11 on November 29, 2001.

Feuerstein never gave up trying to save his 3000 employees' jobs rather than see them migrate to countries with cheaper labor costs. "It would be unconscionable," he said later to one of the many audiences he addressed as an invited and honored speaker.

On August 26, 2003, the company emerged from Chapter 11. On October 7, 2003, the U.S. Congress approved a $19.1 million expenditure for Polartec garments for use in all branches of the U.S. military. To everyone's amazement, Feuerstein once again staved off the apparent inevitable loss of his company by selling undeveloped land adjacent to Malden Mills for $100 million. The courage, compassion, and integrity Feuerstein expressed through his leadership, along with the justice he created for his loyal workforce, has sent ripples throughout the business world. Serving as a beacon for catalyzing positive change, he embodies wisdom that looks beyond the short term and "does what's right" for employees and the community.

In a 60 Minutes interview with Feuerstein on July 6, 2003, Morley Safer commented, "the fact that you became a hero for simply doing the right thing is a terrible commentary on the business world." We prefer instead to see much hope in this inspiring MAD (Making A Difference) example Feuerstein has set for today's leaders.

- When you face a moral challenge and it appears that the easiest way out is to compromise your ethical beliefs and values, stop and imagine yourself standing in front of a mirror. Remember how hard it can be to look into your own eyes or the eyes of those your decisions will most affect if you don't stay true to a higher good.
- Don't forget that the power of your spirit is far greater than the fear created by ego-based emotion. When your own feelings or the reactions of others are set to intimidate you into compromising your ethical standards, draw upon the strength of your deepest and best self to stay the course and do, as Aaron Feuerstein would say, "what's right."

○

Adapted from material originally published in the book, *The Wisdom of Solomon at Work: Ancient Virtues for Living and Leading Today,* by C. Manz, K. Manz, R. Marx and C. Neck (Berrett-Koehler, 2001).

Charles C. Manz, Ph.D., is a speaker, consultant, best-selling author, and the Nirenberg Professor of Business Leadership at the University of Massachusetts. He is the author or co-author of over 100 articles and 17

HAVE A HIGHER PURPOSE

books, including his five Berrett-Koehler books : *The Leadership Wisdom of Jesus (1998), The New SuperLeadership (2001), The Wisdom of Solomon at Work (2001), The Power of Failure (2002),* and the *Foreword Magazine* Gold Award winner for best self-help book of the year, *Emotional Discipline (2003).* His two newest books are titled *Fit to Lead* and *Temporary Sanity.*

Karen Manz is a writer and speaker in the areas of spirituality and work life and adult learning. She has co-authored articles in a variety of journals and periodicals. She is a co-author of the books, *The Wisdom of Solomon at Work: Ancient Virtues for Living and Leading Today (Berrett-Koehler, 2001)* and *For Team Members Only: Making Your Workplace Team Productive and Hassle Free (AMACOM, 1997).*

Robert D. Marx, Ph.D., is an associate professor of management at the University of Massachusetts and is a member of the faculty of the Athens Laboratory for Business Administration, Athens, Greece. He is co-author of *The Wisdom of Solomon at Work: Ancient Values for Living and Leading Today (Berrett-Koehler, 2001)* and *Management Live! The Video Book.* He has won numerous teaching awards and consults with many organizations in the United States and Europe.

A Caregiver Who Cares
by Steve Ventura

She's neither a business executive nor a community leader. You won't read about her in the papers, she's done nothing for "the masses," and it's unlikely that she'll ever receive any type of public award. But five days a week, in her own small and quiet way, she makes a big difference for the people she touches. Her name is Lucy. And she is—as she's so proud to say, even after twenty-five years—a NURSE.

Nurse Lucy works day shift in Postpartum—the place where new mothers are cared for after giving birth to their truly special miracles. And those patients who—by luck of the morning assignments—have her as *their* nurse, are in for large doses of the one medication she's allowed to prescribe: TLC.

If you could peek at the scores of thank-you letters and commendations in her personnel folder, you'd know that Lucy is from "the old school." She believes that providing the absolute best patient care possible is the only *real* agenda. As a result, she has (by her own admission) had some difficulty adjusting to today's cost-cutting "business approach" to healthcare. More patients per nurse, increased documentation, limited (read non-existent) overtime, belt-tightening restrictions on the use of supplies, and a never-ending barrage of new regulatory-driven policies and procedures are just a few of her professional realities—ones that could interfere with tending to *her* new mothers if she'd let them. But she doesn't.

Lucy understands that nursing is about taking care of people. As a result, she somehow always finds the time to remake a bed (for the third time) so a patient will be a just little more comfortable, or make someone's day with a sponge bath and back massage, or have a comforting chat with an anxious new mom, or hunt up a treat for a hungry visiting dad—even if it means occasionally cutting into her own lunch time to do it. "I know that hospitals can be scary and expensive places," she told me. "I just try to help my ladies have a positive experience . . . and get their money's worth."

The behavior of this difference maker is guided by three simple principles that seem applicable to anyone—regardless of their occupation or industry:

- Despite any challenges you may be facing, never lose sight of your ultimate purpose—the real reason your job exists.
- Strike a balance, but occasionally be willing to put the needs of those you serve before your own.
- Pay attention to the little things—the random acts of kindness that add up and mean so much to those on the receiving end.

That's what she does; that's how she creates so many magical moments for those she truly cares for.

Yes, her name is Lucy. And she is—as *I'm* so proud to say, even after twenty-eight years of marriage—my wife.

○

Steve Ventura is an author, educator, and training program designer. His books include *Walk Awhile In MY Shoes, Forget For Success, Start Right . . . Stay Right,* and *Who Are THEY Anyway,* co-authored with BJ Gallagher.

FIND
COMMON
GROUND

Behaving Leaderfully
by Joe Raelin

It strikes me that people make a difference when they behave
leaderfully in everyday life. By leaderfully, I'm not suggesting that
they get out in front of the pack to distinguish themselves.
Rather, that they fit into the pack and, often, by mere example,
serve to bring people together. In *Creating Leaderful Organizations,*
I talk about a former student of mine named Keith, who as a
Peace Corps volunteer, demonstrated this inclination in words
and deeds. In my class he seemed wiser than his years in our classroom dialogue, especially when it came to questions of individual
agency. He found the cowboy mentality of the new titans of
industry in our MBA class to be ill-suited for the webs of relationships characterizing our twenty-first-century organizations.
He was the one most inclined to point out, for example, the dark
side of charisma. That it could be as much a tool to manipulate

for self-serving ends as a basis for engaging a community. He was far more interested in how people could draw others together to collaborate for the greater good.

Subsequently, he wrote in his journal about an instance in his Peace Corps work that may have predisposed him to leaderful practice:

> It would have been easy for my farmers to simply learn and enact the projects that we were working on and not to share their knowledge with others. However, every one of my farmers actively sought out others with whom to share their new knowledge. They did this, not for me, but rather because they understood why I was there working with them, and they believed in the value of the project. They knew that the more far-reaching the project, the more far-reaching the benefits for all.

Keith was apparently able to impress his farmers with the power of collaborative action. From him, we can all learn that people can do together what they may not see themselves capable of doing as individuals.

M.A.D
TIPS

- Demonstrate that leadership can arise and benefit from all members of a community.
- Draw meaning, not from your own mind, but from the sense of the community as its members work together.

- Realize that leadership can be a social, mutual phenomenon.

○

Joe Raelin holds the Asa Knowles Chair of Practice-Oriented Education at Northeastern University where he is also director of the Center for Work and Learning. He is the author of *Creating Leaderful Organizations: How to Bring Out Leadership in Everyone,* a treatise on the power of collective leadership.

Restoration: Healing Relationships by Healing the Earth
by Storm Cunningham

Restoring a horribly polluted, trash-choked river with badly-eroded banks is a challenge under the best of circumstances. Now, imagine tackling such a project located between Israel and the Palestinian Territories. Flowing from the Palestinian city of Nablus, through Israel to the Mediterranean Sea, the Alexander River once seemed a lost cause. Today it's an oasis of green in a parched, degraded area, and wildlife is rebounding.

The fish in the Alexander River never heard of war, suicide bombers, or Middle East turmoil. They simply died quietly in the stinking sewage and heavy pollution that filled the river for half a century. But Nachum Itzkovitz—the three-term Mayor of Emek Hefer Regional Council—heard the fish crying and saw them dying. In 1995 he chose Amos Brandeis, an architect and regional

41

planner specializing in complex, large-scale environmental projects, to plan and manage the river's rebirth. Itzkovitz established—and Brandeis managed—the Alexander River Restoration Administration, comprising twenty public and state entities in Israel from the local to the national level.

The Ministry for the Environment, the Jewish National Fund, the Emek Hefer Regional Council, and the Sharon Drainage Authority spent over $12 million on the restoration. New and renovated water infrastructure on the Israeli side removed most pollutants, and environmentally friendly methods of flood protection were used. Seven river parks were created, attracting thousands of people every weekend. There's an annual River Parade, and the public is involved in saving the huge and rare Nile Soft-shelled Turtles.

The economy was also rejuvenated: Entrepreneurs developed leisure activities near the river parks to serve the 200,000–300,000 visitors who come from around the country to see the restored river. The contractors who worked on the Palestinian side of the project are all Palestinians, and the German funds supporting that part of the project were important to the Palestinian economy. The restoration of the stinking sewage ponds that border the residential areas of the Palestinian town of Tul Karem increased both quality of life and real estate values. The Israeli people of Emek Hefer and the Palestinian people of Tul Karem ignored painful political issues to heal the environment, creating an inspiring example for both their peoples. The project received five prizes, including Australia's 2003 International Thiess Riverprize.

All around the world, thousands of rivers and urban streams are being restored for wildlife, for aesthetics, for flood control, and for socioeconomic revitalization. This is just a tiny part of the fast-growing, trillion-dollar-a-year restoration economy. Restorative development (defined as socioeconomic revitalization based on restoring the natural and built environments) is replacing our old frontier-style new development model, which is based on conquering new land and extracting virgin resources.

How can you *do* such work? Almost every population area has groups devoted to the revitalization of watersheds, ecosystems, historic areas, agricultural lands, and estuaries. If yours doesn't, find something you'd like to restore, and start one: You'll find restorative projects to have uniquely bipartisan appeal. At the national and international levels, public and private professionals, scientists, non-profit leaders, students, and citizens are joining organizations like the Revitalization Institute (www.revitalizationinstitute.org) to foster restorative development of our communities and natural resources. They provide Restorative Governing training for communities and government agencies, and can assist your local efforts.

The Alexander River Restoration Project shows what can happen when public and private interests integrate the restoration of the natural, built, and socioeconomic environments. Such work often has a restorative effect on its practitioners, as shown by the Alexander River experience.

M.A.D
TIPS

- Many times, natural and cultural resources are shared by two or more parties that have social, political, or ethnic differences. Such conflicts—even when at a much lower level than that of Israelis and Palestinians—often result in the degradation or destruction of these shared resources. If your primary goal is the healing of human conflicts, you might find that creating a restoration initiative for these damaged resources—when done in a collaborative manner—will produce the social results you seek . . . as a by-product.

- It's said that people will work hard for three things—money, a leader, and a cause—with money being the least powerful motivator and a cause being the most powerful. Many organizations—business, political, nonprofit, and spiritual—have good people, and sometimes even good leadership, but find themselves stuck fast, unable to accomplish much. This historic shift from destructive, frontier-style development to growth based on revitalization offers myriad restorative causes around which organizations of almost any type can reorient and revitalize themselves. What could be more inspiring than restoring our world?

○

Storm Cunningham is the author of *The Restoration Economy (Berrett-Koehler, 2002)*.

LEAD EARNESTLY

Making A Difference, One Person At A Time

by BJ Gallagher

While some people make a difference by transforming whole organizations, others do it in a quieter way. They reach out to help others, one person at a time. Jim Shaffer is one of those people. He was the chief financial officer at the *Los Angeles Times* where I worked in the late 1980s.

My first two weeks with the company were spent in orientation, beginning with individual meetings with all the senior executives. I was a few days into this orientation when I met Jim in his office. He was warm and friendly, handsome and outgoing, his boyish good looks giving him the appearance of a twenty-something junior executive, rather than a forty-something CFO.

He asked me how I liked my job so far, and I responded enthusiastically. "What's not to like? Smart people, interesting work, great pay, and a high status organization—what more could a girl want?"

He smiled knowingly and reached for a piece of paper. On it he drew something like a diminishing cosine curve: morale on the vertical axis and time on the horizontal; morale starting very positive, then declining to negative before recovering to a lower positive.

"Let me give you a little heads up," he said. "When you come here, you're excited, optimistic, full of energy." He pointed to the top of the cosine curve. "Then, when you've been here a while, you start running into obstacles. It isn't quite as wonderful as you thought." He points to the curve heading downward. "It keeps getting worse, as you encounter bureaucracy and get frustrated. Finally, you hit bottom." He pointed to the bottom of the curve—then he circled it. "When you get there, call me. We'll have lunch."

"OK, thanks," I said. "I'll do that."

Several months went by, and sure enough, Jim was right. My experience was exactly the way he had predicted. Finally, I picked up the phone and told him: "I'm ready for that lunch."

"I wasn't expecting your call so soon," he said over lunch. "I thought I'd hear from you in a year or so . . . but three months?"

"I'm a quick study," I replied unhappily. I poured out my tale of woe, alternating between tears and anger. He listened; he nodded; he shook his head sadly. He was able to empathize and tell me I wasn't crazy. He was also able to help me see options and choices—I didn't have to be a victim of the bureaucracy.

What I learned later was that I was not the only young manager whom Jim had coached through difficult times. He had a whole cadre that he watched out for and helped develop. He loved to spot bright, young, talented newcomers and work with them one-on-one. He understood how important individual attention is in a huge organization. He made a difference in the lives of each and every one of us.

The biggest difference Jim made was simply by taking an interest. It made us feel valuable to have a senior executive take the time to encourage us. I'll always be grateful for the difference Jim made in my life, and I know that many others feel the same.

Ask yourself these important questions . . .

- Is there someone in your workplace who could benefit from your coaching, mentoring, and encouragement?
- If you were going to advise newcomers on how to be successful in your organization, what would you tell them?
- What might *you* gain from becoming a mentor to bright, young, rising stars where you work?

○

BJ Gallagher is a consultant, speaker, and author, specializing in diversity, personal accountability, values and ethics, and gender issues in the workplace. Her clients include the American Press Institute, the *Arizona Republic*, the *Atlanta Journal Constitution*, and Gannett newspapers, among others. She has co-authored three Berrett-Koehler books: *A Peacock in the Land of Penguins* (2001), *What Would Buddha Do at Work?* (2001), and *Customer at the Crossroads* (2000). To learn more, go to www.peacockproductions.com.

LEAD EARNESTLY

Rebuilding Workplace Trust
by Michelle L. Reina

Lori Brown dedicates her professional life to the care of sick and gravely ill babies and children. She is the vice president of Regional Services for Children's Hospital and Healthcare System of Milwaukee.

The hospital was invited to take over the pediatric care services of a smaller hospital. In the business world, this might be viewed as a merger. Mergers often create problems. In the healthcare field this is particularly true.

Caring for others in a hospital is demanding: healthcare providers often feel overextended and underappreciated. In fact, they burn out and often leave the field. In spite of these challenges, Lori was excited about expanding her leadership role to this hospital. With a small staff of 110 people, she saw a chance to create an environment where people trusted one another and were excited about their work.

However, she was shocked by the level of distrust that existed. She saw finger pointing and blaming, gossiping and backbiting, terse and abrupt communication, new ideas shot down, a wall of resistance, and people resigning.

Lori's priority was to rebuild trust. This would take healing and understanding of the dynamics at work. She knew it would be hard and that she could not do it alone. She harnessed the expertise of her CEO, hired an organizational development consultant and an executive coach. Lori drew upon a trust-and-betrayal model to help her understand the many dynamics of trust, betrayal, and healing.

It was clear that she needed to teach her people about trust and healing. Providing this kind of education in healthcare is tough. Since the patients come first and require constant care, it is virtually impossible to bring staff together with any degree of regularity. How could she provide her people with the tools and knowledge necessary to rebuild trust if she could not get them in the same room?

She got creative. She provided her people a pioneering web-based community building tool that allowed them to come together, to engage in dialogue about trust and healing, every-day—*anytime, anywhere.*

With this tool, Lori and her people fully observed what had happened via the merger and the day-to-day ways they treated one another. Lori listened carefully to how her people were feeling. She heard their uncertainty about how they fit in and about their future with the hospital, she heard their feelings of vulnerability about having a new leader they did not yet understand, and she heard about the loss of relationships because of staff leaving.

She asked them what they needed from her and each other, and paid attention to their answers. She shared her own feelings of vulnerability, as well as her sadness and disappointment about the way she saw people treating one another.

Does trust get broken in this hospital today? Sure it does. Yet, Lori and her people have learned this is a natural part of rela-tionships. When trust is broken, they pay attention. They observe what has happened, talk about their feelings constructively, shift from blaming to exploring options, and take responsibility for making changes. They practice trust-building behaviors and monitor them regularly.

- We may value trust, yet it is our behavior that builds it. Practicing trust-building behaviors is everybody's job.
- Betrayal of trust is a natural part of relationships and may strengthen an organization when worked through appropriately.
- Organizations can use technology to bring people together for sustainable trust building.

○

Michelle L. Reina, Ph.D., is a speaker, consultant, and principal of Chagnon & Reina Associates, Inc., *Trust Building Experts*®. She is the co-author of *Trust & Betrayal in the Workplace: Building Effective Relationships in Your Organization* (Berrett-Koehler, 1999). Reach Michelle at www.trustinworkplace.com.

Someone You Should Know
by Dick Axelrod

People with graduate engineering degrees don't expect to walk the picket line. But that is what you would have seen in February 2000 when over 14,000 Boeing employees went on strike. The largest white-collar strike in U.S. history. Today, despite slumping aircraft demand and layoffs, employee satisfaction is at a ten-year high.

Many leaders following a strike would try to remedy the situation by implementing strategies with sophisticated control systems to manage change from the top. But not Hank Queen, Boeing's vice president of engineering and product integrity.

What Hank did was to apply three simple beliefs.

The first is that people accomplish more when they work together. So he engaged a wide spectrum of employees and union leaders in developing a new direction. What came out of those discussions was the desire "to create a work environment where people could be successful." But working together was not limited to developing the change strategy, it was at the very heart of what he asked his organization to do.

The second is that success requires people to be engaged in the new direction. This meant involving more people than ever before and giving local units the freedom to decide what changes were needed.

The third is that if people sit down and talk with each other about what bothers them they will make decisions that benefit themselves and the company. Hank put this belief into action by asking leaders to discuss three questions with their work groups, and to take action based on those conversations. The questions were:

What is your current job satisfaction level?

What is most important to you about your job?

What are the biggest issues or greatest barriers to improving your organization?

By asking leaders to engage in these discussions, he addressed employee satisfaction in a simple yet profound way. Hank did not tell people what to work on, or even how to address the issues. He believed that the answers would come from the conversations.

However, Hank's trust was not blind. What he expected was that the discussions would occur. And, he backed up that expectation by making employee satisfaction a key component of performance reviews.

Hank didn't let people flounder. He used his power to make sure that time, training, and consulting resources were available to help employees and managers address these questions.

What sets Hank apart from other leaders is that he doesn't just give lip service to working together. He includes others, he sets challenging goals, he establishes clear limits, he provides people with the resources to get the job done, and then he gets out of the way.

- Don't do it alone. Engage employees at all levels in identifying what needs to change and in changing it.
- Make sure the work is worth doing, not just to you but to everyone involved.
- Help people focus on the task by providing a few clear boundaries.
- Provide local autonomy so people can decide for themselves how to reach the goal.

- Make available the time, resources, and training necessary to do the job.

○

Dick Axelrod is the co-founder of the Axelrod Group, Inc., a consulting firm that pioneered the use of employee involvement to effect large-scale organizational change. He is the author of *Terms of Engagement: Changing the Way We Change Organizations (Berrett-Koehler, 2000)* and co-author of *You Don't Have to Do It Alone: How to Involve Others to Get Things Done (Berrett-Koehler, 2004).*

Speaking up
by Emily Axelrod

I often hold back when an idea pops into my head. Mother taught me to be polite and let others go first. Many women were taught not to speak up because it was unladylike.

Mary Ann Bobosky has taught me to speak up about what I am passionate about.

Mary Ann is passionate about providing high quality public education. She speaks with conviction at civic meetings in her community. She talks with large businesses such as Lucent and Argonne National Laboratory to form partnerships to support teachers and students. She helped spearhead a committee that got a tax referendum passed in a community where 65 percent of the residents did not have kids in school, the community was in an economic downturn, and 75 percent of the referendums in the state had failed.

She speaks from experience with a lilt in her voice and a smile on her face. She is not punishing; she is informing. She is not critical; she is educating. She doesn't weigh you down with guilt; she gives you the facts.

She is a parent-involvement guru. She advocates for parents to be actually involved, not just informed. She wants them on the school committee that makes decisions about curriculum and other important matters for their children. Mary Ann made parent involvement work in her district and now she travels around the country helping other districts understand involvement and partnering. She doesn't just speak up at official meetings; Mary Ann speaks up at parties and in everyday conversations. She doesn't miss an opportunity.

We can learn from Mary Ann to speak up for what we are passionate about. We can speak up where we work, and in the communities where we live. We can speak up about issues that impact us, we can speak up about things we care about. When we speak up, we make a difference to ourselves and those around us.

- Speak up about what you are passionate about.
- Educate without being critical.
- Put energy into maintaining relationships.

○

Emily Axelrod is the cofounder of the Axelrod Group. Emily speaks up with southern wit and charm. She is a contributing author to Peter Block's *The*

Flawless Consulting Fieldbook and Companion (Jossey-Bass/Pfeiffer, 2000). She is the co-author of *You Don't Have to Do It Alone: How to Involve Others to Get Things Done (Berrett-Koehler, 2004).*

Mike, the Barber, Shapes Lives as He Cuts Hair
by Donald Mitchell and Carol Coles

Mr. Michael Cogliandro has proudly served Harvard students, employees, and professors in any way he could. When he learned that many poor students couldn't afford hair cuts, he would cut their hair for free. If you were a little short, he would say, "Pay me when you can." At Christmas each customer would receive a beautifully wrapped gift, whether or not they paid for their hair cuts.

Mr. Cogliandro also listened carefully to his customers and would ask them about their families, backgrounds, studies, work, and cares. Because English was a second language for him, if he didn't understand something he would keep asking questions until he did.

And he never seemed to forget a single thing anyone said. He sometimes realized that he had information that would help his customers. But why should they listen to a humble barber? Mr. Cogliandro became a master of the Socratic method, asking questions to help hearers learn. Many would report that it was like taking a Ph.D. oral exam on one's own life.

When he moved his shop near to Harvard Law School, his

old customers trekked up to see him. Many of his new customers were law professors and law students, who used the Socratic method in class. With this added practice, Mr. Cogliandro sharpened his skills. Over the years, his clientele grew to include many of the most prominent Nobel laureates, deans, politicians, judges, physicians, and foundation heads in Massachusetts, all of whom valued his wise questioning.

Mr. Cogliandro began to share even more information by helping customers meet and learn from other customers. He built a new community among his customers in the process.

When his partner decided to retire, Mr. Cogliandro carried on. Over the years whenever someone was sick, Mr. Cogliandro had always driven to their home or hospital to cut their hair. Why not provide a mobile barber shop that goes to homes, offices, and even airports? This mobile service has been a delight to customers ever since.

He later found employment in a unisex salon that had replaced his shop, making his female customers (whom he had served for years) feel more comfortable. When he retired from that shop, his customers held a huge party for him, hosted by a Nobel laureate at the Harvard Faculty Club, that exceeded the gatherings most deans receive when they retire.

Mr. Cogliandro never met a person he didn't want to help. If he heard that a customer had died, he would be among the first to call the family to express his condolences. If a customer's family member or friend needed help, Mr. Cogliandro worked on the problem, just as though it were his own. He would ask every customer what they thought the person in trouble should do, until useful answers emerged. Then he would call the person to share

what he had learned. To Mr. Cogliandro, everyone is a stakehold-
er who deserves help from Mike the barber.

- Ask people you meet questions about themselves to understand their situation, their capabilities, their needs, and
  how they learn.
- Find out more about how to help people with these situations, capabilities, needs, and learning styles by asking
  experts who you meet.
- Introduce people to experts and ask questions that help
  them realize what they need to change in order to improve
  their lives.

○

Excerpted from *The Ultimate Competitive Advantage (Berrett-Koehler, 2003)*.
Don Mitchell and Carol Coles are co-authors of *The Ultimate Competitive
Advantage (Berrett-Koehler, 2003)*. They are also the co-authors of *The Irresistible
Growth Enterprise (Stylus, 2000)* and *The 2,000 Percent Solution (AMACOM,
1999)*.

Every Child Deserves A Home
by Stewart Levine

Gail Johnson has spent her professional life working as a children's advocate, including twenty years finding permanent families for children who lost families through abuse or neglect. Her early success recruiting and preparing families to adopt children with medical, emotional, and developmental disabilities often ended in the frustration of being told such children were unadoptable.

Tens of thousands of children were languishing in the California foster care system, out of reach of the adoptive families they desperately needed. The stakes were high. Within two years, over 50 percent of foster youth who emancipate without a permanent family are homeless, in prison, or dead. With perseverance and a steady focus on the vulnerable children, she led the state to radical adoption reform. California no longer considers any child unadoptable, and Gail is leading a new collaboration with the state to find permanent families for the hardest-to-place children—foster teens.

Gail is the Executive Director of Sierra Adoption Services, a private nonprofit agency whose mission is to transform the lives of foster children by finding and nurturing permanent adoptive families. She credits her success to a willingness to challenge the policy makers with "Why?" The California child welfare system was based on a set of assumptions that simply were not true. How could a child be unadoptable if there were families qualified and willing to adopt them?

When Gail faces conflict with bureaucrats she tells them she knows they are in this line of work for the same reason—they care about children. She invites them to consider another point of view, and help her understand their perspective. She designs services to make their jobs easier. When she is successful, she gives credit to the bureaucrats. She has changed California foster children's chances to have a permanent family. Her ability to make a difference is her belief that the only person she has the power to change is herself. So she focuses on how she is part of the problem, and invests in learning how to change herself.

I resolve conflict and create partnerships for a living. Gail called me in 1999 when Sierra was engaged in a federally funded partnership known as Capital Kids Are Waiting with a county child welfare agency. The working relationship had fallen apart because of their historical differences and the lack of a clear agreement for results. Gail wanted to resolve both the long and short-term conflict, get beyond mistrust, and forge an effective high performance team. Few people believed the working relationship could be salvaged. The conflicts were resolved, but more important, a working agreement was structured that provided the foundation for solid, healthy working relationships, and a new vision of collaborative partnership. In the year following, 109 children previously considered unadoptable and destined for a life of foster care were placed in permanent homes.

Gail quickly admits that the process helped her see her part in the problem, one that she was blind to. She realized she had been making the same mistake most people make in situations of conflict—looking for what others were doing wrong and never exploring the ways in which she might be contributing to the

LEAD EARNESTLY

situation. She was not the only one to see their part. Change happened across the board because Gail had the courage to admit her part in the conflict. Her vulnerability helped the vulnerable children she serves. Because Gail got MAD, thousands of kids have homes and families they otherwise would not.

- The first questions to ask yourself in situations of conflict are "What am I doing or not doing that is contributing to the conflict?" and "What do I have to do differently?"
- It is always important to remember the mission of a project or organization so you keep what's important right in front of you as a way to maintain perspective and keep you focused on the goal.

○

Stewart Levine is the founder of ResolutionWorks. He forms teams and joint ventures in a variety of difficult situations. He works with individuals, couples, partners, and small and large organizations of all kinds. *Getting to Resolution: Turning Conflict into Collaboration (Berrett-Koehler, 1998)* was an Executive Book Club Selection; featured by Executive Book Summaries; named one of the Thirty Best Business Books of 1998; endorsed by Dr. Stephen Covey, and featured in *The Futurist* magazine. *The Book of Agreement (Berrett-Koehler, 2002)* has been endorsed by many thought leaders and called "more practical" than the classic *Getting to Yes*.
Information: www.ResolutionWorks.org.

POSITIVELY M.A.D.

Building a Collaborative Nation
by Stewart Levine

John Bartels is a South African lawyer who wants to make a difference. He is the Legal Officer of the Nelson Mandela Municipality. Before South Africa's first democratic constitution of February 1997, John provided "large city" input about the laws that would facilitate the transition to democratic local government. After the new constitution, there was public discussion to give detail to the vision for democratic local government. John played a large role at both a municipal and a provincial level—arranging workshops to explain, listen, and consolidate input. His efforts contributed to a white paper on local government.

The new constitution requires laws that facilitate the building of democratic local government with a strong emphasis on developmental activities. These laws provide for boundaries, structures, systems, finance, information, and promotion of justice. Because John felt so strongly about the potential for local government to heal some of the wounds of apartheid, he was deeply engaged in the process of law-making. He was tireless in giving presentations on the new legislation to previously disadvantaged people new to democratic local government.

John helped people to understand that the new South African constitution:

1. Requires municipalities to cooperate with one another in mutual trust and good faith by fostering friendly relations;

assisting, supporting, consulting, and coordinating actions
and legislation with one another; and avoiding legal pro-
ceedings against one another;

2. Requires Parliament to support intergovernmental relations; and provide for mechanisms to facilitate resolution
of intergovernmental disputes;

3. Requires municipal government agencies to settle disputes
without going to court;

4. Requires local government to provide: accountable government for local communities; services in a sustainable manner; social and economic development; a safe and healthy
environment; encouragement for community involvement
in government organizations; and

5. Requires that a municipality organize all of its activities to
give priority to basic community needs while promoting
social and economic needs at a national and provincial
level.

Peter Gabel, professor of contract law, said that my book,
The Book of Agreement, "begins from the premise that the purpose
of agreement is to build a bridge to the 'other' and to realize your
common aspiration for connection. Writ large, this idea would
. . . help to realize our spiritual nature as social beings in pursuit
of mutual affirmation."

John Bartels read *The Book of Agreement* and believed it could
provide great value for South African municipalities. He believed
the new constitution created a beautiful vision for local government, a vision that needed to be implemented in a new way. He
had a sense that municipal government could become a driving

force—facilitating both positive change for the future and reparations for people disadvantaged in the past.

John believed that "the provisions of the South African Constitution require mandatory processes that would benefit greatly from the 'Agreements for Results' approach." He decided that the contracting process for his municipality must not be adversarial—it must be about creating new visions for the future. He is using the Agreements for Results approach during the negotiation and crafting of municipal contracts, with very encouraging results. He wants to teach all contracting officials in his municipality to use the Resolutionary form of Agreements for Results in all contracts. He is seeking permission from the Municipal Council to train municipalities all over South Africa!

I was introduced to John when he emailed and asked if I had a certification program. I said no and he said he wanted to create one. He keeps reporting progress and I know I will be traveling to South Africa to certify a team of Resolutionaries. Why? Because a lawyer named John Bartels was MAD.

M.A.D
TIPS

- Never doubt the power and vision of your own thoughts—if you can think it, you can achieve it.
- Lawyers can be good guys.
- Great adversity can lead to lasting significant change. The post-apartheid vision may generate a new paradigm we will all be following.

○

Stewart Levine is the founder of ResolutionWorks. He forms teams and joint ventures in a variety of difficult situations. He works with individuals, couples, partners, and small and large organizations of all kinds. *Getting to Resolution: Turning Conflict into Collaboration (Berrett-Koehler, 1998)* was an Executive Book Club Selection; featured by Executive Book Summaries; named one of the Thirty Best Business Books of 1998; endorsed by Dr. Stephen Covey, and featured in *The Futurist* magazine. *The Book of Agreement (Berrett-Koehler, 2002)* has been endorsed by many thought leaders and called "more practical" than the classic *Getting to Yes.*

Information: www.ResolutionWorks.org.

MOBILIZE
COMMITTED
PEOPLE

MAD For Global Justice
by Charles Derber

In 1999, I flew cross-country with five of my Boston College undergraduate and graduate students to participate in the legendary Battle of Seattle, a huge protest against corporate-driven globalization. Our spirits soared with the excitement of the festive crowd, the stirring speeches, and the colorful marches. But the bright sunny day was soon darkened by thick tear gas and armored military vehicles on the streets of that beautiful city. When we came back to Boston, we all felt Seattle had been an historic event and we decided to bring the Seattle spirit into the heart of our own university.

A few months before our trip we had started a small campus organization called the Global Justice Project (GJP). Then we made several presentations to the campus about Seattle, and suddenly much larger numbers of students—sometimes 100 or more—showed up at meetings. They were mostly new to politics but many had gone on Jesuit service missions to Appalachia or Central America. They were moving from service to activism. Their favorite topics: sweatshops, global warming, human rights, transnational corporate power, the WTO, fair trade, vegetarianism, animal rights, sexuality—issues of justice in every arena.

The GJP bloomed into a network-based justice movement driven by the raw hunger of students to learn and make change. I became a housekeeper: securing rooms, contacting speakers, getting a bit of funding from the administration. I also offered some intellectual guidance about the complex issues of the global economy. But mainly I found that my role was to stay out of the way and let the students gain confidence in their own change-making skills.

The organization sustains itself today as a decentralized network, driven by smaller groups and individuals with a MAD passion. A student comes into a meeting and talks about fair trade coffee initiatives she is taking; within five minutes, a list goes out for others to sign up and help. Two students talk about protecting indigenous water rights in Bolivia; another list is circulated and other students sign on. In just an hour, ten different initiatives are introduced and backed by the larger network. The focus is on getting the work done rather than on endless talk.

GJP is now six years old and it has turned Boston College into one of the most activist campuses in the nation. For me, the lesson is that significant change can be achieved by planting a few seeds and getting out of the way.

I'll bet that you also have people in your organization—workers, peers, executives—MAD for justice. To help them get going, suggest discussion or reading groups, bring a little food, support a field trip or two, encourage their initiatives and then ride the wave they create. Restrain your own tendencies to manage or guide the group. You'll be amazed at how they can run their "MAD for justice" show on their own!

- Believe in young people's capacity to change the world, even when they don't believe in it themselves.
- Don't let your own authority get in the way of the initiative of people who are supposed to look to you for leadership.
- Let your passion for justice override your instinct to follow the rules.

○

Charles Derber is professor of sociology at Boston College. He is author of nine books including *Corporation Nation (St. Martin's Press, 2000), The Wilding of America (Worth Publishers, Inc., Second edition, 2001),* and, most recently, *Regime Change Begins At Home: Freeing America From Corporate Rule (Berrett-Koehler, 2004).*

MOBILIZE COMMITTED PEOPLE

A Stone in the Water
by Marvin Weisbord and Sandra Janoff

In the spring of 1991, OD (Organization Development) consultant Marilyn Sifford cornered Marv at a local Philadelphia Region OD Network meeting. "A bunch of us are connected to a social action group," she said. "We would like to learn future search." She was referring to an impactful planning meeting that Marv had described in his 1987 book *Productive Workplaces* as one of a few methods he knew for "getting everybody improving whole systems."

"Well," said Marv, who had been experimenting for ten years, "I'm not sure it's teachable. You have to learn by doing."

Marv and Sandra, with whom he had run future searches since 1988, met with a group that included Marilyn, Carol Cohn, Ralph Copleman, Jean Haskell, Marti Kaplan, Ferne Kuhn, and Skip Lange. Together we planned an action research project. The consultants would donate their services to needy nonprofits. The two of us would mentor them for free. We would discover if people with minimal training could run successful future searches. We defined success as enabling systems to do things on Monday considered impossible the Friday before.

Soon sixteen consultants had recruited sixteen local nonprofits and twelve successful future searches were run. In no time people were calling from Washington, New York, Toronto, Ottawa, Denver, Los Angeles, and Seattle asking if they too could learn and serve. In 1992 we set up Future Search Network with

120 founding members. Our pro bono training program soon led to more than 100 planning conferences in health care, education, community development, congregations, housing, sustainability, and the arts.

Word got around. Katherine Esty and Gil Steil took future search to Bangladesh, from whence Kim Martens carried it to Pakistan and Thailand and Sharad Sapra to Iran and the Sudan. Mike Bell took the process to the Inuit of the Arctic, Tony Richardson to the aboriginal peoples of Australia.

Soon we were raising money for the Network by training people on five continents. By 2004, more than 3000 people had learned the process, and 350 people from twenty countries belonged to Future Search Network. Anyone could join by signing a learning agreement (on the basic principles) and a service agreement (to do pro bono work and share learning with others). Alone we could do very little. Together we had a global change strategy that anyone could join. Moreover, we were a global community bound together by our commitment to serve society.

Today FSN manages future searches anywhere in the world for whatever people can afford. Members have helped improve water quality in Bangladesh, demobilize child soldiers in Sudan, control AIDS in Tanzania and South Africa, stimulate economic development in Northern Ireland, improve school district planning across North America, facilitate cross-cultural business mergers in South America, train women leaders in Siberia, promote interracial cooperation in many cities, revitalize religious congregations, and upgrade health care in communities everywhere. Tens of thousands have been involved. On a shoestring budget with a part-time staff, the network has become one of the most highly-leveraged social change agencies anywhere. The stone cast by a few local people in the Delaware Valley thirteen years ago now makes ripples around the world.

- Join Future Search Network (set your own membership fee).
- Join a worldwide neighborhood of committed others dedicated to a more open, equitable, and sustainable society.

○

Marvin Weisbord and Sandra Janoff are co-directors of Future Search Network and co-authors of *Future Search: An Action Guide to Finding Common Ground in Communities and Organizations* (Second edition, Berrett-Koehler, 2000). See Future Search at www.futuresearch.net for their workshops on managing future searches and on facilitating large, diverse groups.

Heeding the Call: The Practice of Peace
by Peggy Holman

I've never been a peace activist. In fact, despite living near Washington, DC during the October 1969 march to end the Vietnam War, I was away hiking. Yet here I was hosting a conference of 130 peace builders from 25 countries to "expand the field of possibilities for peace within organizations and communities; between nations; and within ourselves."

My involvement began two years earlier, when four random emails, three from strangers, arrived within days . . .

- Harrison Owen, a friend and creator of Open Space Technology (OS), wrote of 25 Palestinians and 25 Israelis gathering in Rome;
- A story came of OS in Kashmir;
- Another OS story with Kurds; and
- A query on using OS to address violence in Colombia.

I connected these remarkable folks by e-mail.

Fast-forward a year:

Harrison Owen offered to bring his Practice of Peace workshop to Seattle in 2003. I pictured the potential for people from different conflicts gaining insight about their situation through others. MAD as it seemed, with no background in peace activism, I invited the OS peace builders I knew, making the leap that their costs could be covered.

Then I asked for support. Bringing Arabs and Jews from Israel, people from Haiti, Colombia, Bosnia and Herzegovina, Northern Ireland, Burundi, Nigeria, U.S. urban communities, Canadian First Nations, Nepal, India, and others was no small undertaking. Colleagues jumped in to help.

So began a serious experience in manifestation. Our planning meetings opened with silence, reflecting on the higher purpose we served, giving the work meaning, and keeping spirits and commitment high. Whatever obstacle we faced, our needs were

71

met. When donations became critical, a professional fund raiser arrived. Through many challenges, trusting each other and the universe, from marketing to music, it came together.

Participants said the conference changed them. Already beyond anger, many worked through grief. Tova Averbuch, an Israeli guest, said it well:

"Gradually I realized that maybe the main point isn't for the Israeli version to be heard but rather for something within myself to move, and the movement took me by surprise. From despair and horror, grew recognition that we are only one, small place. There are better and worse situations than the Middle East. I always knew it in my head but this time the heart understood and began translating that understanding into steps of creating strange ways to see shades of light."

Violence in Nigeria and Burundi were averted because of practices participants brought home. Plans for conferences are underway in Nigeria (for warring tribal youth), New Mexico (where conflict bubbles beneath the surface), Kashmir, and Colombia.

What made this possible? Is it repeatable?

It is repeatable and possible for anyone. Pay attention to your inner call; speak from passion and commitment; ask for support. That will enlist others. Together we moved the practice of peace into the world, attracting remarkable people. You can do the same, whenever you are moved to act. The call for peace sounds around the world. Join us: www.practiceofpeace.com.

What calls to you?

M.A.D. TIPS

- Listen to your inner voice and take responsibility for what you care about most deeply.
- Commit to bringing your passion to life, inviting others to join you. Passion is a remarkable attractor.
- Continually revisit and refine the purpose that guides you, individually and collectively. It keeps the spirit and energy to do the work alive.

○

Peggy Holman consults with organizations and communities to increase their capacity for achieving what is most important to them. Her work encourages people to take responsibility for what they care about, resulting in stronger organizations, communities, and individuals. Her book, co-edited with Tom Devane, *The Change Handbook: Group Methods for Shaping the Future (Berrett-Koehler, 1999),* has been warmly received by those wishing to improve their organizations and communities.

An Avalanche of Change
by Moshe Yudkowsky

Bear with me a moment. Although what I'm talking about sounds very geeky, there's an important lesson to be learned.

You know how frustrated you get when your software doesn't

work? Well, it's even more frustrating for me, because I know a lot about software and given half a chance I could fix it myself. And that's lucky for me, because while all the software I use is top-notch, at the same time I have access to the source code of the software—all the secrets of the software, neatly laid out so that I can fiddle with it if I want to. In fact, if I want to, I can improve it and resell it. *And* most of the software is completely free of charge.

Top quality software at no charge? Software that I can *change* when it doesn't work the way I want it to? Software that I can modify and *resell?* Most of the Internet runs on this kind of software, and it's started an avalanche of change that has swept aside many of the old ways of creating software. How can this possibly work?

Twenty years ago, a group of extremely talented software engineers were faced with a quandary: They loved to write software and share their work, but the evolving corporate model stifled their creativity by imposing severe restrictions on sharing—secrecy, patents, and licenses. They responded with a fascinating and radical innovation, "open source" software. Members of the open source movement make their source code—the fundamental building blocks of the software—"open" for anyone to read, copy, modify, and (sometimes) resell. They've broken apart—disaggregated—many traditional aspects of ownership, surrendering them to the public at large.

What's the result of making source code open? Disaggregation of ownership is based on *sharing,* and the consequence of sharing is more sharing. Let's say I want an error fixed or an improvement made. I don't just complain; I try to do it myself. And because disaggregated ownership creates a *communi-*

ty, I feel responsible to the community. I release my fixes and improvements to everyone else, and thousands of other professionals do the same. This constant stream of community improvements makes open source software extremely reliable, highly secure from viruses, and very useful; the famous Linux project literally has hundreds of thousands of talented developers.

So the result of this radical sharing is . . . *even more sharing.* Engineers love to tinker and make improvements, and disaggregating ownership removes the barriers that prevent them from contributing. Disaggregation's benefits are enormous: creative software, synergy between different software projects, specialized software . . . The list goes on.

- Examine the traditional notions of what you must own—both material things and processes—and what ownership means.
- Sharing begets sharing. Disaggregate ownership and let others contribute.
- Transform your customers into a community and they will surprise you with their willingness to contribute.

○

Dr. Moshe Yudkowsky is president of Disaggregate, a company that creates technological change. Moshe is author of *Avalanche! How Your Technology Can Lead the Next Revolution,* to be published in early 2005.

Sucker Punched to Save the Amazon
by John Perkins

You might say that Bill Twist was sucker punched into heroism. He is a hero among tribes deep in the Amazon rain forest but it hit him unexpectedly.

In 1995, Bill was a successful San Francisco businessman. His wife, Lynne Twist, was one of the nation's top fund raisers (and author of the highly acclaimed book *The Soul of Money,* published in 2003). I was working with the Shuar, an Amazon tribe most famous for shrinking the heads of its enemies. I had known the Shuar since my Peace Corps days in the 1960s and during the early 90s helped them preserve their forests. Their neighbors, the Achuar, hearing of our successes, asked me to assist them in their struggles against the oil companies that threatened to destroy their way of life.

I called on Lynne. She convinced nine people to let us guide them into the jungle. Bill went along to accompany his wife. By the time the trip ended, those nine people had contributed $118,000 to help the tribe begin mapping its territory. Bill agreed to "temporarily" oversee the disbursement of the funds. Like a man sucker punched, he had no idea what was coming.

The plight of Amazon cultures became Bill's passion. He and Lynne founded The Pachamama Alliance (TPA), a 501(c)(3) nonprofit. By 2004, TPA had raised and donated several million dollars to the Achuar and other Amazon tribes. The organization has provided legal, accounting, mapping, and other technical help, given them dozens of two-way radios enabling remote communities to communicate with each other, purchased a small airplane, and financed the training of pilots and mechanics so they can respond to emergencies. TPA has probably done more than all the foreign aid combined to keep the tribes from taking up arms against the oil companies, while at the same time waging political battles to force the companies to stay off tribal lands.

Bill's management of TPA has worked miracles. Yet, his most important contribution is one we can all make: He has committed his heart and soul to making a difference in the world. He has acted and, in so doing, serves as a model and inspiration for all of us.

Bill is not an anthropologist or social worker, not the sort of person you would expect to find sloshing through the jungle with headhunters. He had no special training for this type of work. However, he saw something that opened his heart. I like to say he was sucker punched, but the truth is that a brief trip woke him up to a reality he had never before witnessed. And he took action.

Bill's story is every person's story, including yours. It is the story of a person who saw the need for change and decided to make it happen. Bill is a true hero. His story calls each of us to action, to be MAD, to make a difference.

M.A.D
TIPS

- Look at the world around you with new eyes, see things that you have not discovered before where change is needed, and commit to taking actions that will create the required changes.

77

- Understand that we are all interconnected and make a point to better educate yourself about the role you and the corporations and government that serve you play in the world community; also commit to sharing this knowledge with others.

○

John Perkins is the author of *Shapeshifting, The World Is As You Dream It, (Destiny Books, 1994), Psychonavigation, The Stress-Free Habit (Inner Traditions International, 1999),* and *Spirit of the Shuar (Destiny Books, 2001).* His newest book, *Confessions of an Economic Hit Man,* will be published by Berrett-Koehler in November 2004. To learn more about John, go to his Web site: www.JohnPerkins.org. To discover more about the work of Dream Change, the 501(c)(3) nonprofit he founded that is transforming global consciousness, visit www.dreamchange.org.

A Model for Expanding Goodness
by Donald Mitchell and Carol Coles

In 1968 Millard and Linda Fuller gave away their worldly possessions and began working with Clarence Jordan at Koinonia Farm in Georgia to develop the seed of Habitat for Humanity International, a nonprofit, ecumenical Christian ministry that provides decent housing to help eliminate poverty and improve family life. Donors provide land and capital, volunteers and the families buying the homes help with the building, and the houses are sold at cost with no-interest mortgages to deserving families. Since that time, more than 125,000 homes have been built in over 80 countries.

From 1973 to 1976, the Fullers succeeded in testing the vision in Zaire, where Mr. Fuller established an ongoing organization to achieve this vision. This has allowed others to pursue the vision more easily, learn to proceed, and attract partners.

Drawing on his expertise in marketing, Mr. Fuller soon developed a number of ways to interest others in supporting Habitat, including writing books about the experiences, sponsoring fund-raising and volunteer-attracting walks, speaking at churches, and holding special building day events.

The organization soon split into affiliates to operate in accordance with the Habitat vision and model, each responsible for finding resources, volunteers, and families to purchase and assist in the building. Affiliates were encouraged to donate one-tenth of their funds to support home building in other countries so the program could be expanded into poor countries where the needs were greatest.

Habitat for Humanity International (HHI) encouraged individuals and organizations to establish their own initiatives. Since 1984, former U.S. president Jimmy Carter and his wife, Rosalynn, have sponsored and participated in an annual event to build houses, and their example helps attract ever-growing publicity, volunteers, and donations. HHI also loosened its control over national affiliates, so that these organizations could adapt the vision to better fit their own countries, stimulating changes that led to even faster and more successful growth. And, the organization improved in designing lower-cost housing, training inexperienced builders, and organizing the building process.

As Habitat for Humanity International has grown, the quality of the benefits to all stakeholders has improved as well. The sense of satisfaction is greater now for volunteers and donors because they see and hear more signs of success, communities and neighborhoods benefit from having more of these new homes clustered together, families become stronger from having had decent homes for a number of years and enjoying more physical security in neighborhoods with other Habitat families, and children living in the Habitat homes help one another do better in school.

Unexpected benefits resulted. Habitat families banded together to oust neighboring drug dealers. Volunteers developed new skills and self-confidence, sometimes even leading to new careers. Donor churches became stronger spiritually. New friends were met. Marriages among Habitat volunteers are not unusual.

A unique element of the Habitat innovation experience is that sheer enthusiasm for the organization's purpose, its "why," helped drive many of the innovations. This enthusiasm is built upon the joys of being a servant leader.

- Seek to live the ideals you believe in by making their accomplishment your daily focus and show others how living their ideals will improve their lives.

- Find ways to help people help themselves to meet their most urgent needs.
- Constantly improve the ways you use to help people help themselves by providing lots of autonomy and the inspiration to look for better solutions.

○

Excerpted from *The Ultimate Competitive Advantage*.

Don Mitchell and Carol Coles are co-authors of the *The Ultimate Competitive Advantage (Berrett-Koehler, 2003)*. They are also co-authors of *The Irresistible Growth Enterprise (Stylus, 2000)* and *The 2,000 Percent Solution (AMACOM, 1999)*.

Ingredients for Making a Difference
by Robert Jacobs

Federal, state, and local funding cuts make for tough times for arts organizations. Downturns in the economic cycle mean decreased contributions. Arts organizations become luxuries. They are forced to make do with increasingly smaller budgets and staff. This is the challenging environment where Joh Broughton positively made a difference.

When she joined The Performance Network in Ann Arbor, Michigan, fifteen years ago, it was home to a number of different people and theatre groups. Each had its own interests. The organization, in Joh's words, "was run so each of these people could do

MOBILIZE COMMITTED PEOPLE

their own thing." One wanted political theater. Another was obsessed with Beckett and experimentation of form.

"One of the best things about The Network when I joined was that they'd let you try anything," she explained. "It was a place where I could learn from knowledgeable and wacky people. The problem was that the organization could not survive this way financially. It held the possibility of making a great contribution to the community. But it was only a possibility because in those days, it wasn't clear that The Network would survive at all."

At the time, the theatre produced a variety of plays on minimal budgets. Amateur actors made do operating out of a cramped warehouse with a pole in the middle of the seating area. The theatre's debts were mounting. The programs were facing cutbacks. Day-to-day survival was the norm. Growth was not even a word in the vocabulary of those who worked at The Performance Network.

One day the board and staff of the theatre decided it was time to think big. They put together a ten-year strategic plan to transform the theatre. During the next decade, Joh spearheaded this effort supported by scores of others. She kept the vision in front of people. She connected the theatre's creative roots and this powerful vision. Her energy, enthusiasm, and commitment to creating a lasting institution inspired others to join the cause. Some made financial contributions. Others volunteered their time. Slowly the shared vision began to unfold.

Today The Performance Network has become the only professional theatre in Ann Arbor. Housed in a beautiful new play space, the company has won many regional awards for the quality of its productions, even earning national acclaim from playwrights and critics.

These tips were used by Joh to make a difference in her world. They can easily be applied to make a difference in your world too.

- Invite others to join you.
- Dream big.
- Connect your vision of the future to the organization's past.
- Keep that vision front and center over time.
- Let your energy, enthusiasm, and commitment inspire others.

○

Robert W. "Jake" Jacobs is founder and president of Robert W. Jacobs Consulting, a firm specializing in accelerated, sustainable change. He is the author/contributor to four books including *RealTime Strategic Change* (Berrett-Koehler, 1994) and *You Don't Have to Do It Alone: How to Involve Others to Get Things Done* (Berrett-Koehler, 2004). You can visit Jake on the web at www.rwjacobs.com.

Strength and Determination on the Pampas
by Sharif Abdullah

The economic collapse in Argentina reached Western headlines in December 2001 but devastated that country's rural heartland well before that.

Luci de Cornelis and her family faced economic ruin when they could not make the bank payments on their farm. After exhausting all of their economic alternatives, in 1995 they faced the bank's foreclosure date. As if things needed to get worse, on the eve of the bank's foreclosure auction, Luci's husband had a stroke from the strain and social embarrassment.

"I did not know what to do," Luci said to me as we sat outside at her friend's Argentine ranch on a cool fall day. "I prayed for help."

The day before the auction was to take place, Luci found herself at the local radio station, telling her story into the microphone, asking someone, *anyone,* for help.

She got help. The day of the auction hundreds of women from neighboring farms showed up, blocking the auction. Without anger and without violence, they joined together and stopped the process. They employed innovative tactics: the women sang hymns and prayed—so loud, they drowned out the auctioneers! They linked arms, forcing the auctioneers to push through a line of mothers and grandmothers.

The women found strength in numbers. What seemed to be a personal tragedy was really a social movement in the making.

Through their informal network, they have saved over 1,000 ranches from auction, over 1,000 families from financial ruin, just by letting other women know when another family was in trouble. Because of their efforts, over 200,000 hectares of farmland are still in the hands of local farm families.

And they do not stop at just blocking the auction. Instead, the women sit down with the bank and negotiate for more time, better terms, lower interest rates. Sometimes, the banks get just as much as they would have received from the original loan—just over a longer time period.

The women learned a valuable lesson: It is possible to create a "win-win" situation in even the most out-of-balance circumstances. Before the auction blockages, they were supplicants to power. After the blockages, they were partners with the bank.

Luci could have stopped once her own farm was saved from foreclosure. However, she saw beyond her own personal situation to view the larger context. Her own farm secure, she still works tirelessly for the security of other families, many of whom she does not yet know.

- Call for help: You may be surprised who comes to your assistance.
- Practice absolute nonviolence. "All violence is on the side of the banks. If we tried to resist the foreclosures with violence, we would be crushed."

- Balance the power dynamic: Whenever one side has power and the other does not, there is a situation or condition that can be abused. Instead of seeking "power-over," the women created "power-even." From this position, dialogue and negotiation make sense.

○

Sharif Abdullah is an author and catalyst for inclusive social, cultural, and spiritual transformation. His work as a humanistic globalist has taken him to over two dozen countries and to every continent. His writing includes *The Power of One: Authentic Leadership in Turbulent Times (Consortium Book Sales, 1995)* and *Creating a World That Works for All (Berrett-Koehler, 1999)*. He is founder and president of Commonway Institute.

CAPITALIZE
ON ADVERSITY

Children of Promise
by John Stahl-Wert

The Rev. Dr. W. Wilson Goode, Sr. is an admired and celebrated leader. President and Mrs. George W. Bush consider him a friend, as did President and Mrs. Clinton. University researchers and legislative policy makers cite his impressive results in Philadelphia. And community leaders across the country seek him out to learn how to do in their cities what he does in his.

Dr. Goode's recent national notoriety is the product of a program he birthed called "Amachi." A West-African word that means "Who knows what God has brought us through this child?" Amachi is a mentoring program that serves children of prisoners in the greater Philadelphia area. The most vulnerable of all at-risk youth, children of prisoners stand a 70 percent statistical chance of one day being incarcerated themselves. A caring relationship with an adult mentor changes these odds radically, transforming these children of prisoners into "children of promise," as Wilson likes to say. Hundreds of children in Philadelphia have benefited from Dr. Goode's tireless labors, and thousands are benefiting nationally because of his inspiration to others.

Did Dr. Goode's two terms as Philadelphia's first African American mayor inspire and equip him for this role of great significance? Was it his earlier years as manager of the city that led him to this new role of service? Or perhaps his prestigious degree from the Wharton School of Business gave him the needed impetus. From outward appearances, these prestigious positions may seem to explain what motivated and prepared this man for his current season of servanthood and greatness.

"My daddy was in prison when I was a boy," Wilson himself explains. "And everybody assumed I was destined for a life of unskilled labor at best." He tells this story to a cellblock full of incarcerated men, his eyes warm with true understanding for those before him. He wants these men to permit their children to receive a mentor.

"And I believed what the grownups told me," he continues. "I wasn't college material. And I didn't have much to offer."

The room is now completely silent. The guards in back have started to pay attention; they've never seen this room grow so still.

"But a mentor changed all of this for me," Dr. Goode continues. "A mentor loved me, told me I could become whatever was in my heart to become. And that man's care and encouragement changed the course of my entire lifetime."

Dr. Goode can look back over five decades of satisfying and significant public service, several advanced degrees, and well-deserved accolades. He governed a world-class city and won the

POSITIVELY M.A.D.

trust of presidents. The *greatest* impact of his life will never be measured, however, as thousands of youths, children of promise every one, are diverted from their predicted fate to lives of unfolding goodness.

It was the pain and the hardship of Dr. Goode's life, converted into compassion for others like himself, that made his greatness possible. Pain and hardship—qualities abundantly available to us all—converted into compassion for others. In this way, Wilson Goode is changing the lives of thousands; for them, he may as well be changing the world. In this same way—allowing the hardships we endure to soften our hearts toward others—we can make a true difference too.

- Mentors can positively impact our lives at all times, but during times of adversity they are especially beneficial, so seek them out.
- Look for ways to mentor others, especially those in dire need of attention, assistance, and help.
- Ask yourself what hardships you've endured, and how the lessons gleaned from those experiences might be put into the service of others.

○

John Stahl-Wert is co-author with Ken Jennings of *The Serving Leader: 5 Powerful Actions That Will Transform Your Team, Your Business, and Your Community*

(Berrett-Koehler, 2003)(www.theservingleader.com) in which Dr. Goode's inspiring Amachi story is more fully told. Dr. Stahl-Wert is also president of Pittsburgh Leadership Foundation (www.plf.org), which sponsors an Amachi program for children of prisoners in western Pennsylvania. "You were born to make a difference," Stahl-Wert and Jennings write. "Start today!"

Norma Hotaling, The Sage Project, Inc.
by Jamie Walters

These days, Norma Hotaling has the schedule of an international jet-setter, flying from the International Anti-Trafficking conference in Manila, to a village in India to observe a former brothel, to Washington, DC and Sacramento, CA, to provide expert testimony on prostitution and trafficking laws, and back to San Francisco, where she runs The Sage Project, Inc., a restorative justice and healing program she founded in 1993.

When Hotaling speaks about child abuse, prostitution, and trafficking, she does so from personal experience, not just theoretical knowledge. Before founding Sage, Hotaling spent eight years as a homeless prostitute and heroin addict who was arrested more than thirty-five times.

Reaching a pivotal moment when she knew that she would eventually die on the streets—most likely at the hands of a pimp or violent customer—Hotaling entered a rehabilitation program and emerged with a passion to share her story and use her experience to help others make such life-changing decisions. In the process, Sage has gotten the attention of other municipalities who want to replicate its programs, and Hotaling has become an advocate for change.

"Most individuals in the sex trade were abused as children," she says. "They were exploited and trafficked into prostitution by an adult in their life. That's the case for several hundred thousand children in the U.S. Yet, despite the existence of child abuse and statutory rape laws, we have terms like "child prostitute," and children being arrested for prostitution while those who traffic, pimp, and purchase their services are rarely prosecuted."

Hotaling aims to change those statistics, and the beliefs behind them. Sage's programs include the First Offender Prostitution Program—the John School—a restorative justice program aimed at first-time purchasers of prostitution; and a diversion program aimed at children who have been trafficked into prostitution and adults who wish to exit the sex trade and create a healthier life.

Sage offers mentoring, health referrals, alternative healing modalities, job training, and more. The majority of Sage's staff were, at some point, in the sex trade and battling their own addictions. The organization also leads a growing campaign to raise public awareness, knowing that in order to foster the necessary change, they must go to the root of the current system.

Sage has won the Innovations in American Government Award from the Ford Foundation and Harvard; the Peter F. Drucker Foundation award for Innovation in Nonprofit Management, and the Oprah Winfrey Angel Network Award. Sage recently won its first federal grant from the Department of Justice, which will support program replication by other communities, organizational development, and additional outreach and public awareness programs.

Hotaling emphasizes that a key issue is to be mindful of our individual and collective beliefs—particularly when they minimize or dehumanize others—and to take care with our language, so that our words lead to actions that help and uplift, rather than harm.

Find more information about Hotaling and The Sage Project at www.sageprojectinc.org.

M.A.D
TIPS

- Remember that even a seeming nemesis can become a potential ally.
- Share your own or other "real people" stories, experiences, and potential solutions to give a personal face to "process and system" issues.
- Remember that your own model—manner, style, actions—can be a powerful communication tool.

○

Jamie S. Walters is the founder of Ivy Sea, Inc., producer of Ivy Sea Online, and author of *Big Vision, Small Business (Berrett-Koehler, 2002)*. Contact Jamie at (415) 778-3910, jwalters–ivysea.com, or www.ivysea.com.

Fostering the Dreams of Foster Children
by Jamie Walters

Lori Cohee remembers the event that changed her life and put her on the path to founding Foster a Dream, a San Francisco Bay Area nonprofit that seeks to raise awareness and improve the lives of foster children.

Cohee was a twelve-year-old from an affluent family in California's Napa Valley. To outsiders, she wanted for nothing, but a darker story emerged when she was called out of gym class and taken to a county social services office where she was questioned about alleged abuse at home.

After the frightening interrogation, Cohee was taken—with only the clothes on her back—to an emergency foster home. It was the first of six foster homes that she would live in over the next two years. "Five of these foster homes should not have received licenses," she says. "In one, I was never spoken to; in another, I couldn't get a glass of water without asking. I marked my thirteenth birthday without even a card or happy birthday wish. I cried myself to sleep for weeks."

During this time, she attempted to present a façade of normalcy at school, but when she was served a subpoena to testify in court against her parents—without any support system—Cohee attempted suicide.

In her sixth foster home, Lori found the support that helped her begin the long process of rebuilding her self-esteem, sense of identity, and dreams. Not feeling confident enough to go to college, Lori built a successful sales career with a high income.

After sharing her story with a local group in 2002, Cohee gave up her lucrative sales career, and launched Foster a Dream.

"People ask me why I would give up a great salary," she says. "Why not? Helping to save a life is worth far more than $100,000."

Cohee's start-up phase pushed her to the outer limits of both faith and experience. But then she remembered the children for whom Foster a Dream exists: Kids who've been in and out of twenty schools and as many foster homes, 80 percent of whom are in the system through no fault of their own; many won't graduate from high school; 40 percent will end up homeless, drug addicted, or possibly involved in prostitution. Some will escalate to violent crimes.

Cohee says that her story teaches others to persevere through and find purpose in even the harshest experiences, and to reconnect with their soul's calling no matter how far from the path they seem to have wandered. "I want to teach people that no matter what their experience, and no matter who they are, there are opportunities to share that, and to nurture the development, growth, talents, and dreams of those around them—that's what 'foster' means," she says.

Cohee's organization has assisted more than 1,000 foster kids through its mentor program, Pillow Pals, which donates essentials like pillows, blankets, and clothing; and by sponsoring a holiday toy drive and "Adopt a Dream" events to celebrate important milestones in the kids' lives. Learn more at www.fosteradream.org.

- Even the toughest experiences give you expertise that can be harnessed to uplift others.
- A powerful core vision and purpose can carry you over steep challenges.
- When all seems lost, there are people and resources that can come to your aid if they know you need assistance.

○

Jamie S. Walters is the founder of Ivy Sea, Inc., producer of Ivy Sea Online, and author of *Big Vision, Small Business (Berrett-Koehler, 2002)*. Contact Jamie at (415) 778-3910, jwalters–ivysea.com, or www.ivysea.com.

The Will to Make a Difference
by Debbe Kennedy

In recent years, we have all watched once-promising careers go up in smoke. Business life has been changed in ways once unimagined, since the advent of the global marketplace, a fragile economy, outsourcing, off-shoring, layoffs, and the uncertainties of war and terror. Many of us have found ourselves in a funk. In some cases, our *will* to contribute *more with less* has been paralyzed. For others it has been a walk into total darkness. No hope. No sense of purpose. No energy to get up for it all again. How do you make a difference under these conditions?

Once in a great while someone passes through our lives, shedding a new perspective on our capacity to rise up in the face of adversity. They seem to help everyone they touch see their own difficulties from a different perspective. So it is with Bill Tipton. His story is about one man's determination to reinvent himself against all odds. It is one with many fingerprints, emerging from deep within the Hewlett-Packard culture, where a cast of dedicated employees, including Bill, manifested HP's belief that *everything is possible.*

Bill's first years at HP as a customer support engineer were spent building skills and confidence. Then without warning, his life changed drastically. Pains in his stomach landed him in the emergency room. For three months he was in a coma. His wife, Kathy, was encouraged to pull the plug. She refused. Miraculously, he recovered. At the end of seven months, he came home from the hospital unable to walk and totally blind.

When I met Bill, he had one dream: returning to work at HP. By then, he was walking with the aid of two canes and working to recast his life and work as a blind person. This meant learning Braille in short order and expanding his portfolio of skills to land a new job at HP. Bill's pioneering spirit was published in a story on HP's Intranet, reaching employees working in over sixty countries. People were touched. Letters of gratitude and support arrived from all over the world. Bill became a new friend to some. Others cheered across the distance—and just the right ones in HP's family showed up to help Bill fulfill his dream. One day his new business card in Braille arrived in the mail bearing his new title: HP Services Tools Integration Specialist.

In each of us, there is an inner strength. It is that gift we often discover by chance and rarely use to its fullest. It is the one that helps us enlist others in our cause. Bill Tipton's example offers a lesson about the *will* to make a difference. His own words say it best, "The future looks bright. We all need to be adaptable and willing to reinvent ourselves to maximize the value we bring to our organizations. This means building new skills, embracing changes and asking every day, *what can I do to contribute my best?*"

- **Re-ignite the *will* to make a difference.** Use times of adversity as a gift to re-group, re-evaluate, re-create, re-organize, re-consider possibilities, re-invent and re-dedicate yourself to overcome obstacles.
- **Repackage yourself.** Use trying times to take a deep look inside your organization. Imagine ways you can re-invent how you present your products or services.
- **Upgrade your skills.** Expand your portfolio of skills. Add new knowledge to your tool bag. Focus on increasing your value and confidence.

○

Debbe Kennedy is president of Leadership Solutions Companies and author of *Action Dialogues (Berrett-Koehler, 2000)* and the *Diversity Breakthrough! Action Series (Berrett-Koehler, 2000).* Learn more at www.debbekennedy.com.

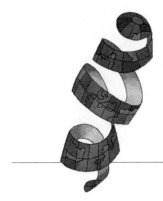

DEFY CONVENTION

Going The Extra Mile
by Ken Blanchard

Making a positive difference in the world, big or small, comes down to sacrifice. I refer to this as the "extra mile" concept. It used to be a Roman law that a soldier could ask a citizen to carry his pack for a mile. Being a law, the citizen had to do it. As the story goes, one day a soldier saw a citizen and said, "Would you please carry my pack?" The citizen not only carried the soldier's pack one mile, but carried it an extra mile as well. The impressed soldier asked, "Why did you go that extra mile?" The citizen replied, "The first mile was for the state, and the second mile was for you."

My father applied the "extra mile" concept in his life. He graduated from the Naval Academy in 1924. The leaders of the country thought we had just fought the war to end all wars—World War I—and they did not think we needed many officers.

So my father was released from the Navy after his senior cruise. He entered Harvard Business School in January 1925, and after graduation he began a career on Wall Street, ending up with the National City Bank. His career was going well, and he was being groomed for a vice presidency. Then in 1940, when I was one year old, he came home and said to my mom, "Well, I quit today."

She said, "You did what?"

Dad said, "I told you when we got married that if the country ever got in trouble, I owed it something. Hitler is crazy and it's only a matter of time until the Japanese get in the war, so I rejoined the Navy. I want to contribute. I want to make a difference here." So Dad went from a high-paying job on Wall Street to one as a lieutenant at the Brooklyn Navy Yard.

When Pearl Harbor came, it looked as if he was going to spend the war at the Navy yard because he lacked experience. But my father wouldn't settle for that. He called an old classmate who worked at the Bureau of Personnel in Washington and said, "What have you got for an old fart with no experience?"

His friend called back a few days later and said, "Ted, all I have for someone with your experience is a suicide group going to the Marshall Islands." My father said, "You've got your man." He took command of 12 LCIs—Landing Craft Infantry—whose job it was to protect the Marines and the frogmen landing on the beaches. The fighting in the Marshall Islands proved in many ways to be Asia's version of Normandy. Seventy-five percent of my Dad's men were killed or wounded.

That's the extra mile. That's sacrifice. That's making a difference.

DEFY CONVENTION

- Identify where you have opportunities to "go the extra mile."
- Recall those instances when you've already gone the extra mile. What motivated you? What was the result?
- Remember, going the extra mile often requires making sacrifices. What sacrifices are you willing to make in order to serve others?

○

Ken Blanchard is the chief spiritual officer of The Ken Blanchard Companies and author of numerous books, including *Empowerment Takes More Than A Minute (Berrett-Koehler, 1997),* and *Full Steam Ahead (Berrett-Koehler, 2003)* (with Jesse Stoner).

Soldier Field
by Alex Pattakos

"Man, I never been to a football game before," Carl said, as the group watched the Chicago Bears play on the dayroom's television set. An inpatient at a state psychiatric unit just outside of Chicago, Carl, I learned, was not alone. In fact, none of the patients in his unit—all lifelong residents of the Windy City— had ever seen the inside of Soldier Field.

"So close, yet so far away," I thought to myself as I watched the game on television with the group that sunny afternoon. But as we watched the game on TV, we noticed that many of the stadium seats were empty. Carl asked, "Why can't we go to the game if they have all those empty seats?"

It sounded like a great idea to me, so on behalf of the group, I telephoned the Chicago Bears office to make it happen. "Absolutely not," I was told in a tone that made me feel like I was being viewed as a mental patient too! In no uncertain terms, I was instructed that—even if stadium seats were empty at kick-off time and remained empty for the entire game—the "owners" of the seats retained the rights to them. In short, they could not be reassigned to anyone else, especially to a group of psychiatric patients! How *crazy* we *all* must be to think otherwise.

Then Walter Jacobsen, co-anchor (with Bill Curtis) at WBBM-TV, the CBS affiliate in Chicago, picked up the story. Before we knew it, the case of the disadvantaged mental patients was on the evening news. To his credit, Jacobsen's commentary drew the wrath of his media colleagues and stimulated a plethora of opinion pieces and letters to the editor, both pro and con, in the daily tabloids for several days.

Unfortunately, in spite of the controversy that ensued, the Chicago Bears organization did not relent on its decision. Still, all things considered, the story does have a happy ending. You see, because of the media attention paid to the issue, dozens of Soldier Field ticket holders graciously donated their seats to be used by our group at the next home game. And just being able to witness the joyful faces of the patients, especially Carl's, at a football game in Soldier Field made all of the effort to get there worthwhile. I don't remember who won the game; it didn't matter. However, I do know that day was *priceless!*

Thanks to the attention of a proactive media personality, the generosity of many citizens, and the determination of the staff (and patients) at a state psychiatric facility, some dreams actually came true. If only for a moment, it was like we all, no matter what our personal circumstances, could hear those famous, inspiring words from Walt Disney: "If you can *dream* it, you can *do* it!"

So, go ahead, dream BIG and act "crazy" the next time you face a formidable situation in your own work or life. Unless you try to do something out of the ordinary, you'll never know what really *is* possible. Take it from a very special group of mental patients *and* Chicago Bear fans, your dreams can come true!

- Challenge yourself to "break the rules" even if it means that you may look *crazy* in the eyes of others.
- Help others realize *their* dreams through collaborative and creative actions.
- Don't give up at the first signs of resistance to your idea!

O

Alex Pattakos, Ph.D., is a principal of The Innovation Group, based in Santa Fe, New Mexico, and author of *Prisoners of Our Thoughts: Viktor Frankl's Principles at Work (Berrett-Koehler, 2004)*. For more information, see: www.prisonersofourthoughts.com.

Bake a Cake for the Office Troublemaker

by John Izzo

Almost every workplace of any size has one of them—an office troublemaker. It may be someone who is negative, the one who does not do a fair share, the one who bad-mouths everyone, or the one who is simply out of step.

With few exceptions, most of these people did not start out in this role on the first day of their job. But somehow, somewhere along the way, a shift occurred and whatever innocent affection we felt towards this person and whatever love they felt for the work passed over into disillusionment. How do we recapture that innocence?

My friend, a nurse, told me about such a woman on her team. She was negative, didn't pull her weight, backstabbed others and was, all in all, someone everyone agreed should leave. Some people had tried to give this person feedback, but to no avail.

For months my friend thought about what she could do to get through to this woman. People had tried to tell her to "get with the program" but to no avail. Hard as she tried, all she could come up with was an inexplicable desire to bake a cake for the "troublemaker." She had no idea why this notion had come to her or what baking a cake might accomplish, but the urge was irresistible. The only thing she had ever heard this woman say she liked was chocolate, so she started her day by baking a chocolate cake. She took the finished cake and headed to her home.

103

Arriving at 11:30 on a Saturday morning, you can imagine the troublemaker's shock when she opened the door. "What are *you* doing here?" the woman asked incredulously.

"Well," my friend said, "it is kind of hard to explain. I know you like chocolate and I woke up this morning wanting to bake you a cake, so I did." She held the cake out like an offering to an angry god.

The woman smiled ever so slightly and said: "Well, would you like to come in?"

For the next hour they sat at the kitchen table, ate chocolate cake and talked. They did not talk about the woman's attitude or her behavior towards colleagues; they simply shared small talk and ate cake.

Monday morning the woman arrived at work, the same grumpy person she had been the week before, but with one notable exception—she was nice to my friend. The next day she even brought my friend a coffee to start the day. Over the next few weeks, they slowly became friends to the point where they were able to have a heart-to-heart conversation about the workplace. Encouraged by the friendship she felt with my friend, the woman slowly started becoming more positive, began asking others for feedback on how she could be a better team member, and eventually regained the innocent enthusiasm she had when she started her job. It took months, but it did happen.

Where do we start when everything else we have tried has not gotten through to someone? It seems to me that it must begin with kindness, with the courage to reach out with no expectations at all. It begins when we decide to be the one friend to the friendless, the one person reaching out when everyone else has shut down, the one who will care enough to be innocent again.

- Who in your community or organization is deemed a "troublemaker"?
- How do you typically approach (or avoid) this person? What alternative approaches might you use to better reach this person?
- Who might label *you* a troublemaker? What changes might *you* make to ditch this label?

○

Adapted from *Second Innocence: Rediscovering Joy and Wonder (Berrett-Koehler, 2004).*

John Izzo, Ph.D., is one of North America's most sought-after advisors and speakers on creating soulful, vital workplaces. He is the author of the books *Second Innocence: Rediscovering Joy and Wonder (Berrett-Koehler, 2004)* and *Awakening Corporate Soul (Fairwinds Press, 1997).* Check out his work at www.izzoconsulting.com.

Dr. Kenneth Cooper, M.D.:
Fight the Good Fight for Us All
by Charles C. Manz

One of his colleagues described Dr. Kenneth Cooper, M.D., as just "a good ole boy from Oklahoma" at heart. Dr. Cooper himself has said that he really expected to simply have a relatively small medical practice and perhaps a rather unremarkable life. Instead he:

- Literally wrote the book on aerobics, popularizing this, at the time, revolutionary concept;
- is the founder of the Cooper Aerobics Center—a state-of-the-art campus that houses the Cooper (research) Institute, Cooper Fitness Center, Cooper (medical) Clinic, and the Cooper Wellness Program;
- is founder of Cooper Ventures, Inc. and Cooper Concepts, Inc.;
- developed Cooper Complete MultiVitamins and Joint Maintenance Formula;
- is the personal physician of many CEOs, celebrities, professional athletes, and President George W. Bush; and
- has written nearly twenty books with combined total sales of over thirty million copies.

Nevertheless, it has been a very difficult road to these many accomplishments. For example, given his advocacy of preventative medicine and healthy diet and exercise beginning in the 1960s, he was frequently criticized by the more "diagnose and prescribe medicine or surgery" medical community. In the late 60s, when his best-selling book *Aerobics* was published, many physicians counseled people, especially those over forty, to avoid significant exercise. One expert even proclaimed "the streets are going to be full of dead joggers if people continue to follow Cooper." And when Cooper advocated exercise to help rehabilitate people who have had heart attacks he was viewed by many as being essentially crazy—as an exercise fanatic. Now this practice is part of standard medical protocol.

Despite his best-selling book, his small practice in Dallas initially struggled. His original modest office had only two rooms. And when the medical board in Dallas believed he was endangering lives by using a treadmill to conduct stress tests they even considered censoring him. Feeling discouraged, he seriously thought about discontinuing his medical practice. As he discussed this possibility with his wife Millie, she helped him to remember that he believed with all his heart that his medical practices represented the future of medicine.

Despite his setbacks, Dr. Cooper persisted relentlessly. Most of his originally scoffed-at recommendations have become accepted good health practices and have been endorsed by doctors world-wide. His strong commitment to medical research guided and redefined his medical stance all the way. "I've worn down the critics . . . there are still a few . . . but compared to thirty years ago it's minuscule. We have overwhelmed them with data," he explains.

Dr. Cooper's commitment to advancing ahead-of-their-time

DEFY CONVENTION

ideas and health strategies in the face of huge opposition is an ideal example of MAD. Being willing at times to confront seemingly overwhelming challenges, while serving the best interests of others, may be the key to making the world a better place for all of us.

- When the world and the people in it seem to conspire to force you to compromise your principles and stick to the status quo rather than do what you deeply believe is right, do what's right anyway.
- Let your best light shine so that those connected with your life receive the benefit of your unique gifts and the distinctive contributions that only you can offer to help make the world a better place for us all.

○

Adapted from material that originally appeared in the book *The Power of Failure: 27 Ways to Turn Life Setbacks Into Success (Berrett-Koehler, 2002).* For up-to-date fitness advice based on health principles from the Cooper Wellness Program, see the book *Fit to Lead* by C. Neck, T. Mitchell, C. Manz, and E. Thompson *(St. Martin's Press, 2004).*

Charles C. Manz, Ph.D., is a speaker, consultant, best-selling author, and the Nirenberg Professor of Business Leadership at the University of Massachusetts. He is the author or co-author of over 100 articles and 17 books, including his five Berrett-Koehler books : *The Leadership Wisdom of Jesus (1998), The New SuperLeadership (2001), The Wisdom of Solomon at Work (2001),*

The Power of Failure (2002), and the Foreword Magazine Gold Award winner for best self-help book of the year, Emotional Discipline (2003). His two newest books are titled Fit to Lead and Temporary Sanity.

Delivering Hope To Rural Africa
by Heather Schultz

Rural Africa has issues indeed. Jobs are scarce and, as often as not, the cash economy has collapsed. AIDS devastates entire communities.

But a new day dawns. Excitement is in the air. They begin to come. Walking, many barefoot. One mile. Ten miles. Twenty. Two hundred. Two thousand. Ten thousand. More. Men. Women. Young. Old. Very old. Children. Lots of children. All coming to the music festival. It is a very special annual event celebrating the arrival of the computers, and it's Kenya's only Festival of Traditional African Music.

The festival is held on top of a hill overlooking the coffee and the maize, and farther below, the fields of ground nuts in Tharaka, up against the 12,000-foot Nyambene Hills, amidst Isak Dinesen's Africa. We are not "out of Africa," rather we are smack in the middle of it. Spectacular.

Twenty-seven schools will compete today for prize money. The finalists include Kaaga School for the Deaf, Nkuene Girls School, the Meru AIDS Orphans, and a group of sixty-year-old men from one of the local churches. The old men get special recognition for their jaw-dropping, heart-pounding authenticity. Local oral history and local song and dance now include the computers. The final dance, the Gikuku Kiatho, lifts the entire crowd. The community celebrates the joy of the festival along with the great promise and community pride that come with the computers.

The Canaan Foundation delivers hope packaged in a computer. Since 1998, we have delivered hundreds of used computers, gathered in America, to approximately fifty secondary schools, orphanages, and related institutions, serving tens of thousands of students in Kenya. By design, the Canaan Foundation Trust in Kenya, a sister organization, assumes heavy responsibility for distribution and maintenance. We are creating both a critical mass of computer skill and an economic link with the developed world.

One small step for mankind is education. The more people are educated, the greater their chance to get jobs and to support their families. Computer and information technology are essential to the development of Africa today, but only 1 percent of the world's computers make their way here.

Maryanne Njeri Mukita, student president at Nkuene Girls School, exclaimed, "I think the project is great. I'm happy about it because we get access to the computers and learn how to use them. If you want to work you must know how to use a computer. We are privileged to get the computers."

For us, we get warm smiles, hugs, and the knowledge that we can change the world. For them, school enrollments soar. Test scores rocket up. Jobs are found. Futures exist.

"But there is no electricity in those villages. You can't use the Internet, there aren't even phones. You'll never get the computers through customs. Companies will never bother to give you their used computers. It's too much trouble," they said.

We are currently collecting and delivering several hundred more computers to Africa. Got computers? We'll take them.

- Got a big idea? Do it!
- You really can change the world!

○

Heather Schultz is co-author with Chip R. Bell of *Dance Lessons: Six Steps to Great Partnerships in Business and Life (Berrett-Koehler, 1998)* and *Online Learning Today: Strategies that Work (Berrett-Koehler, 2002)* with John Fogarty. An international consultant and speaker, she is the former president of Tom Peters' company and the executive director of The Canaan Foundation.

Live Your Values
by Cindy Ventrice

The management team at Xilinx, a San Jose, California-based semiconductor company, has built a culture where adhering to their values is second nature. Leading the way is CEO Wim Roelandts.

Xilinx already had a list of values when Roelandts became CEO eight years ago. He wondered, did these values really represent what people cared most about? So he asked. What employees said formed the basis for Xilinx's CREATIVE values:

- **C**ustomer-focused
- **R**espect
- **E**xcellence
- **A**ccountability
- **T**eamwork
- **V**ery open communication
- **E**njoying our work

CREATIVE is a catchy concept. But lots of companies have catchy concepts that are basically meaningless. Roelandts knew he needed to make these values essential. He worked to entrench the CREATIVE concept into the Xilinx culture. Even today, he still talks about these values in every speech he gives, telling stories to exemplify what is working and what is missing. With Peg Wynn, VP of Worldwide HR, he worked to further reinforce these values by establishing a program where employees nominate each other for meeting one of the CREATIVE values.

Again, many companies have CEOs that talk about values. Few work to build a culture where the management consistently demonstrates its commitment through its actions. Wynn describes the way they make decisions as an example of everyday respect. Everyone has their say. They can emphatically disagree. Each point of view is respected. Once a decision is made they all work to implement it.

Xilinx's commitment to respecting employees was really tested during a three-year economic slump that hit their industry. In response to plummeting revenues, other semiconductor companies had cut their workforces an average of over 20 percent. While Xilinx experienced a 50 percent loss in revenue, they chose not to lay off a single employee.

Maintaining their workforce was a conscious decision. Many, including their own board of directors, questioned the choice to avoid layoffs. The executive team met to weigh their options. Things got a little heated, but ultimately they came out with three goals for the downturn: reduce expenses, maintain productivity, and emerge stronger.

They decided that these could be achieved without layoffs. To reduce labor costs, they implemented an across-the-board tiered pay cut. They offered unpaid sabbaticals with a twist— employees kept their benefits and received $10,000 if they spent a year volunteering for a nonprofit organization. They kept layoffs as an option of last resort. For a team that lived its values, it was a matter of integrity.

Employees responded with understanding and loyalty. Some offered to take an even greater pay cut than requested. Through their commitment to retaining their people, even during a difficult time, Roelandts and his executive team strengthened their relationship with every employee, helping them maintain productivity and emerge stronger.

Real values are those we are willing to live with, even when it is difficult.

- Define your values. Know what really matters to you.
- When conventional wisdom is contrary to your values, question conventional wisdom.
- Find ways to achieve your goals without compromising your values.

○

Adapted from *Make Their Day! Employee Recognition That Works*.

Cindy Ventrice is the author of *Make Their Day! Employee Recognition That Works* *(Berrett-Koehler, 2003)*. A speaker, trainer, and consultant with over twenty years' experience, Cindy works with organizations to solve employee morale issues. You can learn more at: www.maketheirday.com.

Payback
by Dave Haynes

Allan Boscacci, president of American Brass & Iron Foundry, in Oakland, California, ran into a dilemma in the late 1990s. The difficult market forced him to find ways to cut costs in order to stay in business. While most other business executives would bow to the norm and make a workforce reduction, Mr. Boscacci felt a loyalty to his employees.

While Allan happened to be the son of the previous company president, one thing set him apart from other business heirs. Rather than just inherit the company and start at the top, Allan Boscacci started at the bottom of AB&I. Over many years, he worked many different jobs within the organization. In that time, he realized that the one thing that was really keeping American Brass & Iron Foundry alive was the people. Everyone from the janitor to the foundry manager all had a job to do that was vital to the survival of the company.

Therefore, when it came down to a decision to fire those people, Allan just couldn't do it. So, with heavy heart, he presented the only alternative he could to the employees and asked for their approval: each employee would have to take a drastic reduction in pay.

Assuredly, the pill must have been a difficult one for the employees to swallow. Allan promised that it would only be for a short time, and when it was all over, he would pay everyone back for their sacrifices. Words like these from a manager are generally met with overwhelming skepticism. However, the people at AB&I were not skeptical of Allan. They knew he understood their plight from the time he had spent with them in the trenches.

A year later, when the profits returned, Allan kept his promise. Not only did he put all employees back to their original salaries, but he also increased their salaries to the level they would have had, had they been receiving yearly raises during the slow times. While it probably would have been wise from an immediate cash flow perspective to stop there, Allan did not. He also gave bonuses to each employee, the equivalent of all the money they gave up during the slow period. Not only were the employees fully compensated for their sacrifice, but the company gave them back double.

While the immediate cost to American Brass & Iron Foundry was high, the long-term payback was much, much higher. Allan was unable to show a real profit that year, but he was able to shore up an amazing amount of loyalty from his employees. Allan's loyalty to the workers, as demonstrated by his willingness to first, preserve their jobs, and second, exceed his original promise, resulted in a double dose of loyalty to Allan from the workers.

Allan Boscacci "Made A Difference" by doing right by his employees first. By prizing each employee's contribution as vital to the company's success, Allan not only was able to get his company through a difficult time, but was also able to build a bridge of trust between management and employees that will be nearly unbreakable in the years to come.

- **Spend time in the trenches.** In order to effectively manage someone doing a job, you must first understand that job. And the only real way to gain that understanding is to spend time doing that job yourself.
- **Put yourself in their place.** Prior to making a major decision, take the time to envision yourself in the position of all those affected by the decision. Try to identify the differences between the way management sees the decision and the way the "peon" may perceive the decision. Visit

www.peonbook.com to learn more about how the average worker might view your decisions.

- **Recognize the peons.** Your people make you great. They all have a necessary purpose at your company. From the janitor, to the receptionist, to the average worker. Be grateful for the work they contribute and respect them for the contribution they make to the company.

○

Dave Haynes is the author of *The Peon Book: How to Manage Us (Berrett-Koehler, 2004)*.

Creating a Graduate School for Sustainable Business
by Jill Bamburg

After twenty-plus years of successfully consulting to Fortune 500 companies on "intrapreneurship," and a short, but lucrative, entrepreneurial stint in the dot.com economy, Gifford and Libba Pinchot were ready to retire.

Actually, Libba was ready to retire into writing. Gifford wanted to do "just one more thing." And so began another one of the productive running dialogues that has characterized their personal and professional partnership for the last thirty years. "In a dyad," says Libba, "you can pull a little more idealistically as an individual because you know the other person has their feet on the ground."

In the current instance, the couple morphed a concept called The General Institute into the reality of the Bainbridge Graduate Institute (BGI), a full-fledged graduate school offering an MBA in sustainable business. The General Institute was more a state of mind than a real institution: It was an expression of the Pinchots' desire to have a nonprofit vehicle for leveraging their skills, talents, resources, and networks "for good." The Bainbridge Graduate Institute, shaped by their cofounder, Sherman Severin, who had previously headed an MBA program at Marylhurst University in Portland, was a specific manifestation of that desire: a business school that integrates environmental and social considerations into every course.

Many of their friends (the present author included) tried to talk them out of it. It was an insanely ambitious idea—even by Pinchot standards! Higher education is not exactly a profitable— or even a break-even—business. It's a highly regulated industry not easily bent to the will of idealistic entrepreneurs without Ph.D.s—or even MBAs. And then there was the sustainability side of things: no one had quite figured that out yet, much less figured out how to squeeze it into the standard MBA curriculum.

No matter. The Pinchots had both preached and practiced innovation and entrepreneurship for so long, they figured they could fill what they saw as a huge gap in the education marketplace. They recruited a handful of idealists to hold down the core faculty and administrative slots, worked their lifetime Rolodexes to recruit a handful of faculty stars, and hit coffee shops, email lists, and their own far-flung collection of friends for student pioneers willing to embark on an adventure in institutional "co-creation."

On the one hand, the first year created a thrilling student

learning community. On the other, it was rocky in all the usual start-up ways: too much work, too few resources, too many mistakes and surprises, too little time, too much emotion, not enough sleep. But lots of learning per Gifford's entrepreneurial dictum: "Faster learning beats better planning."

The second year was smoother. By the time the first group of students graduated in May 2004, the school had begun to build a national reputation. Enrollment was on target for fifty new students; adjunct faculty from around the country were jumping at the opportunity to teach with—and learn from—this new institution; the transition from being founder-led to being professionally managed was well underway.

And Gifford was again beginning to think about doing "just one more thing."

M.A.D.
TIPS

- Never retire.
- Never stop believing.
- Never say never.
- Never say die.

○

Jill Bamburg is a founding faculty member of the Bainbridge Graduate Institute (BGI) and its MBA program director. She is the author of a forthcoming book from Berrett-Koehler on the challenges of bringing mission-driven businesses to scale. She tried to talk the Pinchots out of starting BGI and is delighted they didn't listen to her.

No Problem

by Beverly Kaye and Sharon Jordan-Evans

If only more managers would say this when their employees ask for something special.

> I was so excited about my daughter's singing debut at her high school. She had been taking vocal lessons; she had developed a strong, beautiful voice, and that day was her chance to show it off. She would sing the *Star Spangled Banner* (without accompaniment) during the all-school pep rally at 1 P.M. My boss was excited for me and said, "No problem," when I asked him if I could go watch her. But here's the best part. Upon my return, with videotape in hand, he asked me how it went and asked if I would show him the tape. It was such a small thing but meant so much to me. I proudly showed him the video and beamed as he praised my daughter. He showed support in so many ways that day.

Busy managers don't always realize that little things mean a lot. Since so many families are two-career households these days, everyone is trying to do their best to pay attention to family and to work. If you recognize that and are able and willing to bend when necessary, it will pay off in the end. Employees who feel that their managers recognize the difficult balance *and* trade-offs that are faced on a daily basis will be more committed to their work.

- Think about each of your "star" employees (those hard workers that you simply don't want to lose), initiate a conversation about honoring family needs. Co-create a list of all the possible ways (small, medium, and large) that you can help them achieve their goals. (Sometimes the smallest request makes all the difference.) Select one or two (together) and make it happen!

○

Adapted from: *Love 'Em or Lose 'Em: Getting Good People to Stay.*

Beverly Kaye and Sharon Jordan-Evans have co-authored *Love 'Em or Lose 'Em: Getting Good People to Stay (Berrett-Koehler, 1999),* now available in 17 languages and recognized as the world's best-selling employee retention book. Their latest book, *Love It, Don't Leave It: 26 Ways to Get What You Want at Work (Berrett-Koehler, 2003)* offers "anyone who works" easy-to-implement strategies for increasing job satisfaction. Beverly is the founder and CEO of Career Systems International, and Sharon is the president of the Jordan Evans Group.

Bend Those Rules

by Beverly Kaye and Sharon Jordan-Evans

Here's the story of a manager who questioned the status quo and ended up supporting a talented employee.

> My company had never allowed telecommuting, and I believed it probably never would. One of my top employees asked me if she could work from home two days a week, and my immediate response was no. A month later she sadly handed in her resignation and said she had found an employer who would allow her to telecommute. I simply could not afford to lose her, so I went to my boss and asked if we might bend the rules on a trial basis, offer her telecommuting two days a week, and see how productive she was. She stayed with us, increased her actual productivity by 10 percent and is a grateful, loyal employee. Since then we have loosened our policy substantially and consider telecommuting on a case-by-case basis for any employee who requests it.

Rules are necessary to some degree, especially to effectively operate large, complex organizations. But rules often take on a life of their own. And sometimes they end up stifling productivity and creativity. If your employee comes to you with a request that goes against a policy or rule, are you willing to hear their point? Give it a try? Go to bat for them? Employees who feel they can come to their manager with a solid request for a new way for work to be done deserve to be listened to. Motivation and commitment will increase if you keep that door open.

- Consider an "out of the ordinary" request by thinking about whether you can honor it for a short period of time. Evaluate how the trial works, how it impacts others on the team, and what the barriers might be to extending that test period. Sometimes we leap to a "no" before we even try something out!

○

Adapted from: *Love 'Em or Lose 'Em; Getting Good People to Stay.* Beverly Kaye and Sharon Jordan-Evans have co-authored *Love 'Em or Lose 'Em: Getting Good People to Stay (Berrett-Koehler, 1999),* now available in 17 languages and recognized as the world's best-selling employee retention book. Their latest book, *Love It, Don't Leave It: 26 Ways to Get What You Want at Work (Berrett-Koehler, 2003)* offers "anyone who works" easy-to-implement strategies for increasing job satisfaction. Beverly is the founder and CEO of Career Systems International, and Sharon is the president of the Jordan Evans Group.

SHIFT PERSPECTIVE

Changing the Dance in Somalia
by Barry Oshry

"Today I am very happy for having assisted the signing of the peace deal . . . between Somali factions who have been fighting for almost 14 years . . . My little contribution to the process was: I made a copy of the article you gave me, *The Terrible Dance of Power,* and I gave it to one of the participants in the peace process; he found the article very interesting and made several copies for his colleagues. He called me . . . yesterday saying that my paper made a huge impact on everyone who read it, and asked me to translate it into the Somali language. . . . As you can see, a simple article can make a difference in an intricate process."

This excerpt is from an email from Ahmed Sheikh Mohamed, a refugee from Somalia currently living in Canada, to his colleague, Diana Cooper. On a business trip to Nairobi, he found the Somali Peace Talks were in the final signing process and he felt compelled to make a contribution. His sharing of *The Terrible Dance of Power* with the peace delegates and their sponsors was, in his words, "a huge success" and "a good wake-up call for many Somalis." Since then Mr. Sheikh Mohamed has created the Centre for Conflict and Peace Studies—Somalia, along with a web site that has become one of the most visited web sites around the world for the Somali diaspora and on it resides *The Terrible Dance of Power.*

I wrote *The Terrible Dance of Power* several years ago. When I learned how it found its way into the hands of the Somalia peace delegates, I was stunned. To think I'd almost passed on writing it. I had turned down an invitation to speak on organizational development in international affairs. After all, what did I know on the subject? I was pressed to speak at the conference and write a paper so I did some research and uncovered an archetypal theme or "dance" playing itself out in many of the then-current (as well as present) war zones. Over the years, *The Terrible Dance* has been published in a small organization development journal, staged by the Seattle Public Theatre, and has made its way to college classrooms, all of which has been gratifying. But to think that *The Terrible Dance* had an impact on the peace in Somalia was overwhelming to me.

What Ahmed Sheikh Mohamed did for the country he loved is inspiring. He helped his countrymen to "First, see the dance. Second, to abandon their arrogance and righteousness. And finally, to stop the dance and create a new dance . . . to rebuild what they have destroyed in the last 14 years."

SHIFT PERSPECTIVE

- Often we keep our most strongly held ideas and opinions to ourselves. But shifting perspective, particularly the perspective of others, means giving voice to our ideas. Get your ideas out of your head and into action. It's a great way to make a difference!

○

Barry Oshry is the author of *Seeing Systems: Unlocking The Mysteries Of Organizational Life (Berrett-Koehler, 1996)* and *Leading Systems: Lessons From The Power Lab (Berrett-Koehler, 2004)*. He is the developer of the Power Lab and The Organization Workshop on Creating Partnership and the producer of the prize-winning documentary "Power Lab: Living In New Hope."

Change Your Questions, Change Your Results

Discovering the Power of Self-Questions in Life and at Work

Marilee G. Adams

Many years ago, I had a personal breakthrough in thinking that changed not only my own life but also became the foundation for my work consulting with organizations, leaders, and teams.

Here's what happened.

While in graduate school I received criticism from a professor on some writing and I responded with calmness and curiosity. This amazed me since previously I would have become upset and immobilized. Wondering what accounted for the difference, I learned the answer lay in the *kinds of self-questions* I was asking. Instead of, "Why doesn't he like and approve of me?" I had switched to, "How can I fix this?" and "What can I learn?"

What I discovered that day would evolve into a system of skills and tools that teaches us how to pay attention to the questions we're thinking and asking, analyze them for effectiveness, and change them if better questions would help us achieve better results. We learn to observe our thinking from two divergent mindsets: in *Judger mindset* we ask questions such as, "What's wrong?" and "Who's to blame?" In *Learner mindset* we ask, "What works?" "What's valuable here?" and "What can I learn?" Both mindsets are part of human nature, and once aware of them, we expand our ability to *choose* how we think and relate—and therefore, what kind of results we can expect.

Learner mindset generally leads to creativity, productivity, satisfaction, and success. By contrast, when we focus Judger mindset on *ourselves,* as I did, we develop self-doubt and difficulty accepting even the most constructive suggestions. Focusing Judger mindset on *others* can lead to anger and conflict, for example when we get mired in Judger at work with a colleague or team. This was the problem for Susan, an executive coaching client in a global organization.

Susan thought she would have to leave the job she loved because she found her boss, Phillip, so impossible. We discovered

127

that without realizing it, Susan constantly asked herself two Judger questions: "What's he going to do wrong this time?" and "How's he going to make me look bad?" Phillip obviously didn't have a chance with her.

I suggested a new question that might change Susan's thinking about Phillip. It was, "How can I make my boss look good?" Though Susan was shocked at the suggestion, she was thrilled with the results. A few months later she had gotten both a raise and a promotion! Moreover, this new Learner self-question led her to refocus her efforts in a more creative and constructive way in general. She and Phillip began co-leading a project team, and through their new collaboration, resolved a productivity problem that had plagued the company for months.

By changing her self-questions, Susan initiated positive changes everywhere in her job. Her orientation shifted from one of "answers and opinions" to one of "new questions and curiosity." She learned to "accept Judger and practice Learner." She told me she always remembers this lesson: great results begin with great questions.

- Pay attention to the questions you're asking yourself—are they helping or hurting you? How could you change them?
- Observe, with empathy, whether you or others are operating from Judger or Learner mindset in any specific situation.

- In the spirit of "accepting Judger and practicing Learner," what Learner questions could help you get better results— at work and at home?

○

Marilee Adams, Ph.D. is a partner with The Center for Inquiring Leadership and the originator of QuestionThinking™, a methodology for transforming thinking, action, and results through powerful question asking. She is also the author of *Change Your Questions, Change Your Life: 7 Powerful Tools for Life and Work (Berrett-Koehler, 2004).* To learn more about the Center for Inquiring Leadership, go to www.CenterforInquiringLeadership.com.

The Good Samaritan
by Debbe Kennedy

I dashed out of a parking garage, mindlessly rushing down the street, acknowledging no one, only to be abruptly halted by a red light. I stood impatiently, grinding my heels into the curb, ready to leap out in front of the crowd at the first sign of *green*. As the light changed, an unexpected slow motion took over. My shoes tried unsuccessfully to hold me back—the heels now solidly stuck in the crevice at the edge of the curb. My body instead took over, looming forward, lifting itself through the air, then falling with a thump onto the street. The point of impact was an excruciating, jolting crash of bones as I landed on the asphalt on both knees. Next, still in slow motion, out of nowhere, came a warm hand reaching out to me. I grasped it firmly, welcoming the care and strength from this person I had not yet seen. As I lifted my head up, my eyes met the eyes of the *Good Samaritan*. My anguish was clearly mirrored on his brown face. *"Are you all right? Let me help you,"* he said without words.

My life was suddenly interrupted as I was literally "brought to my knees," stripped of my dignity, then lifted up and mentored by a man with no place to go. He was homeless. For that moment so was I. I had passed him many times, always much too busy to notice him—or was it just easier to look away? I never heard his voice; never wondered what he had to say or thought about what he needed. I never recognized our sameness. Amazingly, he had time for me when I showed up unannounced.

One seemingly unrelated event—a few chaotic moments in time—shocked me into a new level of understanding and thinking about what it means to make a difference. The nameless man caused me to start asking myself some deeper questions and now I ask you:

- How many times have you rushed by the opportunity to learn from someone else, to broaden your perspective, to recognize a person's contribution to you?
- How many people have you unintentionally ignored in your work and life?
- How many ideas, insights and talents have you overlooked because of your own limiting labels and biases?
- How well do your own actions and behaviors set an example for others about making a difference?

Our organizations would be better places to work if they brought out the qualities of the *Good Samaritan* in all of us. These qualities ask more of us as individuals. They call us to cultivate a genuine interest in the well-being of others that goes a step beyond the organizational core values that are commonly, and sometimes casually, recited—trust, respect, teamwork, innovation, excellence, integrity, and customer service. A young manager brought this to life for me in an interview not long ago. It was clear from my own observations that he was routinely ridiculed and ignored by his seasoned peers and truly struggling to get his bearings in his new role. He had been "brought to his knees" plenty of times. He mentioned none of this to me. Instead, when questioned about what he thought would improve the organization most, he said, *"What if you could come to work every day and know that everyone around you was interested in helping you be the best you could be. Wouldn't that be a great place to work?"*

- **Focus on the small things you do.** Seemingly small unconscious behaviors, actions, and habits can work to exclude people. If you want people to feel valued, notice they exist—say *hello* for starters. Listen to them with genuine interest.
- **Invite others into the process.** If you want people to feel included, bring them into the process of mainstream decisions and activities. Together we can do amazing things.
- **Set the example for respecting others.** If you want people to feel respected, show it. Keep appointments.

SHIFT PERSPECTIVE

Return calls and emails. Give them your undivided attention when they speak. Talk with people when you don't
need something. Reach out to lift others up when you have
the opportunity to make a difference.

○

Debbe Kennedy is president of Leadership Solutions Companies, and author
of *Action Dialogues (Berrett-Koehler, 2000)* and the *Diversity Breakthrough! Action
Series (Berrett-Koehler, 2000)*. Learn more at www.debbekennedy.com.

Facing Economic Reality
by William E. Halal

Sue was the CEO of a company that was struggling with the typical bureaucracy that plagues most organizations. For instance,
the Information Technology (IT) department exceeded its budget year after year. To make matters worse, the line units that used
IT complained constantly about long delays, shoddy work, and
unresponsive techies. Sue repeatedly attempted to solve the
problem by controlling costs, limiting usage, and replacing IT
managers, all to no avail. She was stumped for an explanation.

We introduced a different perspective of "internal market
economics" that helped solve the problem, literally within days.
Most managers have been raised on traditional hierarchical
thought, so they don't seem to realize that organizations are fun-
damentally economic systems. From a market economics view,
the problem became quite clear.

On the demand side, IT costs were skyrocketing because the IT unit was subsidized by the CEO, so it was offering *free goods*. It was a typical cost center and line units could order IT systems at no cost.

On the supply side, it also became clear that the IT unit was not performing well because it enjoyed a *monopoly*. Line units had no choice but to patronize this internal provider, and so the IT manager, Ed, and his employees had little incentive to do a better job.

This analysis led to an incisive solution that was remarkable for its power and simplicity. *The CEO, Sue, simply gave Ed's budget to the line units.* Line units generated this money anyway, so the net effect was to return the *taxes* they paid in overhead to support this *corporate government*. Ed was invited to transform his unit into an "internal enterprise"—just like any small business. He was free to run this business as he thought best, and his unit was permitted to retain all revenue exceeding costs. Ed liked the idea of being an entrepreneur, so he found the challenge exciting. And the line units were thrilled by the prospect of having extra money that they could use to either patronize Ed or buy their IT services elsewhere.

With this shift in perspective, everything changed in days. As some line units began patronizing outside providers, Ed and his people began thinking seriously about how they could improve service to their new *clients*. And now that line managers had to pay with *their own money,* they began considering carefully whether they really needed all the extravagant stuff they once had ordered. Service improved, costs declined, Ed became a celebrated business success, and the line units enjoyed their newfound independence. The CEO, Sue, was delighted to see that some problems could be solved more readily by *facing economic reality.*

This little story illustrates that the basic solution to bureaucracy problems is a fundamental shift to an unorthodox view that recognizes the economic forces driving organizations. We are then faced with roughly the same hard choices the Soviets confronted in the 1990s—should we continue to manage organizations as *planned economies* or should we transform them into *market economies?*

- If you feel confused about some structural feature in your organization, ask yourself how this function would work in an external market economy.
- Remember, unlike a hierarchical organization, there is no right way to design a free-market organization. You can do whatever you think best.
- Don't be frightened by the threat of chaos in a market organization. If you've designed it reasonably well, order will emerge. After all, nobody "manages" the Internet, a market economy, or an ecosystem.

○

William Halal is professor of management at George Washington University, Washington, DC. He is the author of five books, one of which is the source of this story—*The New Management: Bringing Democracy and Markets Inside Organizations (Berrett-Koehler, 1998).*

Listening

by Cindy Ventrice

When expressing dissatisfaction with a relationship, the issue brought up most frequently is a sense of not being listened to. For most of us, being heard is our first priority. Having our problem solved comes in a distant second.

Do you listen carefully? It can make a big difference. Not long ago, I was on the phone with an unfamiliar travel agent. He was very abrupt and was bordering on being rude. His bad attitude was leaking right through the phone lines.

I admit it, I found myself getting annoyed. I considered giving him a piece of my mind. I'm *good* at self-righteous when I want to be. But instead of lecturing him on customer service or asking to speak to his supervisor, this time I took a different approach.

I was quiet for a moment and then said, "You sound upset." I waited. He was quiet for a moment. Then he softly replied, "It's just so frustrating. Several people are out of the office today and the receptionist keeps sending me all of *their* customers, and I have to book thirty flights for *my own* customers before this afternoon."

That was the whole interaction. Twenty seconds, then we finished our business. He was calm and pleasant. I was calm and pleasant. I didn't solve his problem. I just recognized that something was bothering him and then listened. We both benefited. And just maybe, a few other customers benefited from his improved disposition as well.

- Avoid jumping to conclusions. There is often more than one right answer.
- Listen with empathy. Make the other person's emotions at least as important as your own.
- Allow yourself to understand the other person's point of view. Be willing to shift your perspective, if only for a few moments.

○

Cindy Ventrice is the author of *Make Their Day! Employee Recognition That Works (Berrett-Koehler, 2003)*. A speaker, trainer, and consultant with over twenty years' experience, Cindy works with organizations to solve employee morale issues. You can learn more at: www.maketheirday.com.

Overcoming Personal Stereotypes
by Judith H. Katz

Most people think they don't have biases. Often, people who go through educational processes addressing diversity and inclusion think they are aware of their biases. That's the insidious nature of biases. The ones we don't know about are the ones we act upon most often.

I was cofacilitating an education session in which we were exploring the roots of the "isms." We discussed how each of us has a "page 1"—a set of automatic judgments and assumptions that are implicitly learned—often in new situations or in stressful situations our "page 1" appears. One common example that I personally experienced was when I was a child driving through a black neighborhood with my parents and being told to lock the car doors. I learned early on that I should fear black people. It took many years of consciously deciding to build new experiences to be able to create a new set of reactions—to go from fear to engagement. A major step in uncovering our biases is being willing to honestly and deeply examine our assumptions and then being willing to challenge their validity. To do so takes an open mind, a willingness to experiment with new behaviors and to be brave in new circumstances. Our discussion of the hidden nature of biases in the education session had an almost immediate impact.

One of the women from our education group was redecorating her townhouse and was in the process of hiring a painter. Right after one of our sessions, she had an interview that would have turned out entirely differently had it been held a week earlier.

A week before, she might not have even opened the door to the prospective painter she saw on the other side of the peephole. But she had just been talking about examining her biases, and she realized that her instant aversion to the man's multiple facial and ear piercings had all the symptoms of bias. Her normal "page 1" response would have been to judge the man as unprofessional and incompetent based on his appearance alone and upon seeing him at the door would have made up some excuse about changing her mind and not going ahead with the project. Instead she mustered up her courage, fixed a business-like smile on her face, opened the door, and invited the young man in to review his qualifications and approach.

She encountered surprise after surprise. Against all her expectations, she found the young man to be polite, articulate, and highly professional. His resume, portfolio of photographs of previous jobs, and list of references were head and shoulders above anything she had seen from any of the other painters she had interviewed. So she confronted her biases and gave him the job.

To make the story short, he did a fantastic job, and the woman has been actively recommending him to all of her friends and acquaintances—not only will they get an exceptionally professional job, but an opportunity to examine their biases as well. By not following her normal responses, she opened up a world of possibilities and also achieved the quality she desired in a job well done. From this experience she realized the many ways in which her biases were getting in the way.

Because she saw the impact of making this change in her personal life, she decided to challenge her biases at work too. She began to mentor some of the younger employees in the company whom she had previously dismissed. This experience reinforced her new learnings to see past an individual's external appearance and truly seek out what they had to offer. In the end, she brought her skills and perspectives to the younger employees in the company and they gained from her wisdom and experience as well. She was also surprised to discover that she learned new ways of seeing things and tackling problems, and was able to be far more effective in her own role by interacting with many of her young mentees. By taking one small step—opening her mind, her front door, and her office door—she was able to open up a whole new world of experience for herself and to help her organization be more successful also.

We all carry prejudices and biases. The question is how do we let those quick judgments stop us from really seeing what people bring and who they truly are. Some actions that help us to overcome our biases and immediate stereotypes:

- Recognize and fully own your biases—the more we hide from them the more they rule our lives. Step one is to recognize that they are there and to own them.
- Be open-minded: challenge yourself to get out of your comfort zone. Be willing to lean into your discomfort and learn more about the other person.
- Be willing to engage: the only way to break down stereotypes is to get more data on someone so that you see the many facets of who they are, not the one dimension that our stereotypes bring.
- Be curious about the other person: ask questions, seek to understand, and—most importantly—try to learn about their world and experiences.
- Accept the other's frame of reference as true for her or him: other people see and experience the world differently. Whether you agree or not, it is important to learn why they are the way they are.

SHIFT PERSPECTIVE

- Find connecting points: as human beings we all have the same needs—to be loved and to have connection and meaning. We all experience sadness and joy. However, we each may experience these things quite differently. Find the areas of commonality and connection if you want to get beneath appearances and surface assumptions.

○

Judith H. Katz, Ed.D, is executive vice president of The Kaleel Jamison Consulting Group. Judith specializes in integrating culture change initiatives into business strategies of organizations. She is a member of the Diversity Collegium, a think tank of renowned diversity professionals in the United States, and the author of the landmark book, *White Awareness: Handbook for Anti-Racism Training (University of Oklahoma Press, 1978, 2003)*. She is co-author, with Frederick A. Miller, of *The Inclusion Breakthrough: Unleashing the Real Power of Diversity (Berrett-Koehler, 2002)*.

Have the Courage to Seize Opportunities
by Ira Chaleff

How can I make a difference in the world? The question can overwhelm us. It can seem to force us to confront our powerlessness. The world is large and contains endless suffering. We are small and have such limited resources.

But is our world large? Not if we measure it against the galaxy, or the universe. Measured against these, it is barely a speck.

If the world is not large and we occupy a tiny place in this speck of a world, then are we infinitesimally small? Not in relation to the billions of cells in our body, or to the strands of DNA within any given cell that contain the blueprint to make and remake us as an organism.

Maybe small and large are merely viewpoints. Maybe they are not relevant to strategies for making a difference.

I am sure there are people who have pondered their smallness until they could make no difference in the world. But there are also people who pay size and strength little attention and, on the power of an idea, make a difference in the world. Let me tell you one such story.

During the cold war, the U.S. government established Radio Free Europe and Radio Liberty to broadcast uncensored news in different languages to the people of Eastern Europe and the former Soviet Union respectively. Millions of listeners counted on these sources to balance the censored official news broadcast by their own countries.

After the Berlin wall came down, the U.S. Congress reduced the funding for Radio Free Europe/Radio Liberty from $225 million per year to $75 million per year. If "the Radios" stayed in their home in Germany, a very expensive place to operate, they would need to reduce the number of language services they offered by more than half. People in the affected countries in which open news channels were still fragile would be thrown back onto the whims of their rulers.

At this point, people from many levels of the organization and society played a role to make a difference. Three executives of the Radios, deeply troubled by the prospect of dismantling a network of news bureaus and broadcast units that provided a crucial service, challenged their own leadership's plan to reduce programming. They conceived an idea to relocate the Radios to a less-developed eastern bloc country. This would reduce the cost of operating to a fraction of the current budget and permit continued broadcasting in virtually all their languages. This was an act of courageous followership in which loyalty to the organization's mission and stakeholders outweighed acquiescence to the formal leadership.

Supporting this idea was another individual who at one time had been a political dissident lacking any formal power in his country. After decades of maintaining his integrity, the playwright and essayist Vaclav Havel became president of his country, Czechoslovakia. The country peacefully dissolved its federation and become two nations, the Czech Republic and Slovakia, with Havel presiding over the former. This left the federal parliament building in Prague standing empty. Havel, continuing to make a difference, offered it to the Radios for $1 per year if they would relocate there. He knew their presence would continue to consolidate the democratic gains in both his country and the region.

Now it was time for the Radios' board to step up to the plate. Moving the Radios presented management with logistical, diplomatic, legal, technical, and political challenges that most boards would shy away from. Instead of playing it safe, they decided to support the courageous vision and commitment of the Radios' emerging leadership team. They authorized the move, with the proviso that the relatively inexperienced leadership team retain a management consultant to help them with the daunting challenges they faced.

That is how I came to be privileged to participate in this project. For the next six months, I witnessed dozens of nearly heroic acts in which individual team members made a difference: Finding housing for the staff in a city with a severe housing shortage. Migrating from analog to digital equipment in a culture still ramping up its technology. Uprooting one's family to a country that could not provide the services available in the current home. Recruiting new specialists to replace those who chose not to relocate. Working around the clock to ready broadcast studios so language services could be relocated one by one without missing an hour of programming. Supporting the new leadership with a 24/7 commitment to the thousand tasks needed for an orderly transition. Confronting the new leadership when it meddled unproductively with the details entrusted to others.

Occasionally in life we find ourselves in a position to make a big difference with a simple idea and an extraordinary commitment to it. Whether we are a dissident, the president of our country, an organization executive, or down in the ranks as a technician we are not too small to make a difference, provided we are big enough to see the opportunity and courageous enough to take a risk.

The winners in this case? Millions of listeners in Romania, Bulgaria, Uzbekistan, Kyrgyzstan, and other former Soviet-bloc countries.

M.A.D
TIPS

- Initiate new ways of pursuing and protecting a mission you believe in.
- Skillfully build support for your ideas at levels that can champion or veto them.
- Be willing to back up your ideas with commitment, hard work, and sacrifice.

○

Ira Chaleff is the author of *The Courageous Follower: Standing Up To and For Our Leaders (Berrett-Koehler, 2002),* president of Executive Coaching & Consulting Associates, www.exe-coach.com, and chairman of the Congressional Management Foundation, www.cmfweb.org, which develops leaders and their teams in the public and private sectors.

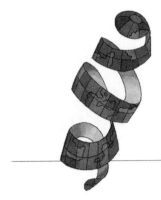

WORK WITH CITY HALL

Joe Taxes
by Don Frick

In 1959, at the age of nine, Joe Gomeztagle immigrated with his family from Mexico to northern Indiana. His parents insisted that he work hard, read widely, get along with people, and make his mark in life by taking responsibility for the whole community, especially "the little people" less fortunate than him. He respected his elders and followed their advice.

In 1991 Joe's neighbor told him she might lose her house because of high property tax bills. He looked into the matter and discovered that Indiana's property tax assessments were wildly inconsistent, even in the same neighborhoods. It was neither fair nor constitutional, but things had been that way since 1851. One tax official told him, "This is only a problem in your township." "That was a lie," said Joe, "but what really made me mad was when a legislator said, 'This is next to impossible to change.' Don't ever say that to an immigrant!"

Joe became an expert on Indiana's arcane tax laws and began a one-person crusade to make a difference. He took vacation days and dropped by the offices of legislators and public officials to chat, ask questions, and share his dream of a better Indiana. He testified at hearings, organized free public forums, gave interviews, and listened patiently and deeply. Some people pulled him into their offices, closed the door, and said, "I can't say this publicly, but keep it up." Others—the true opponents who realized that their empires of power and money were at stake—worked to discredit Joe's motives, but he was not building or protecting any turf or running for office. "The only thing I'm running for is the kitchen table," said "Joe Taxes," as he was now being called.

Even those who were threatened by a change of the status quo could not help but like this unfailingly positive Mexican American who did not come across as a bitter, judgmental tax evangelist but as a fellow seeker who calmly but persistently invited them into a collaborative effort to improve their state. The Indiana Civil Liberties Union and other interested parties soon joined the cause.

The Indiana Tax Court finally declared Indiana's assessment procedures unconstitutional and in 1998 the Indiana Supreme Court upheld the decision. When the legislature adjourned in 2002 without complying with court orders to restructure taxes, Joe took vacation time, donned a heavy jacket, and walked 150 miles from Gary to Indianapolis to publicize the issue. He took no sides on the competing proposals that had deadlocked the two parties; he simply asked that legislators go back and finish their work. By the time Joe Taxes reached the capital city, the governor had called a special legislative session for May where the issue was settled.

Incredibly, this one enthusiastic, dedicated person changed an unfair system that had existed for 150 years. "If you want to make a difference," says Joe Gomeztagle, "don't give up. Learn how to fight by using any negative energy on behalf of the cause."

- Listen to opponents openly and deeply. They are your potential allies.
- Be persistent *and* positive. No one responds well to blanket judgment and condemnation.
- Check your motives. Are they aligned with the common good?

○

Don M. Frick is author of *Robert K. Greenleaf: A Life of Servant Leadership* (*Berrett-Koehler, 2004*).

Find a Way to Say "Yes"
by BJ Gallagher

His presence lit up the classroom the minute he walked in. And his voice—a deep, rich, resonant voice—rumbled out like thunder from somewhere deep in his body, captivating his audience. As he spoke, his face radiated joy and passion for his work, for the people he serves, and for the God he loves. I was spellbound. I had to learn more about this small, golden-brown man with such *huge* presence. Who is he and what is he up to?

His name is Rev. Cecil Murray—Rev. Chip to his friends and fans. He came to the First African Methodist Episcopal (FAME) Church in south-central Los Angeles in 1977, when there were 188 parishioners. Today, they number over 17,000! His secret to success is no secret at all—he will willingly share it with anyone who asks. So I asked.

"My key strategy has never changed—our mission is to take the church beyond the walls," he told me. "Our church is not just someplace that people come on Sunday to worship. We take the message of hope, healing, and love beyond the walls into the community. We work within the system."

"Tell me more about that," I ask. "Working *within* the system. Other religious leaders rail against the system—calling for overthrow of the system, or overhauling the system. That's not what you're saying."

"We work *within* systems that already exist—federal, state, county and city systems," he said. "We partner with groups of all kinds to create solutions for difficult social problems. Things don't happen if you come up against another group and make them wrong. I believe that change comes about by mutual agreement—not by dissent, not by conflict, not by criticizing and judging others.

"I always tell my staff, 'Find a way to say YES.' You can't discover that from a negative place. Be positive. That is what enables us to work *within* systems—to create change from the inside out."

"Can you give me an example?" I asked.

"One of our newest programs is aimed at eliminating gang violence. We have partnered with the LAPD, the SCLC, the ACLU, and other churches to do outreach to gang members and find new alternatives. We don't just sit in our church and pray for an end to the killing. We are out there building bridges between black and brown young people.

"We also have an economic development department where we teach community members how to write business plans, how to apply for loans. We even have an in-house incubator, in which new businesses can get the support they need for up to two years, until they are viable.

"We have an environmental protection office in which we take on problems unique to our community. At one time we were even in the low-flush toilet business, buying toilets and installing them in people's homes. That program, started twelve years ago, turned into a business for two former gang-bangers. We've replaced 20,000 toilets, making a significant impact on the local environment.

"We have over sixty programs, all of which exemplify 'finding a way to say YES.' It's a simple concept that anyone can use in any community or organization. Instead of saying, 'No, we can't do that' or 'No, that's against our policy,' you can simply look for a way to say 'Yes' instead," Rev. Chip summarized as he smiled at me. "Anything else you'd like to know?"

I paused for a second, then asked my final question, "Yes, where can I sign up to join you?"

Ask yourself these key questions:
- What one thing are *you* willing to do differently to find a way to say Yes?
- Can you think of one organizational policy that gets in the way of people working more effectively? What can you do to help change that policy?
- What ways can you think of to take your organization's mission beyond the bounds of "business as usual"—to make a difference to your customers, clients, or other stakeholders?

○

BJ Gallagher is a consultant, speaker, and author, specializing in diversity, personal accountability, values and ethics, and gender issues in the workplace. Her work has been featured in the *Los Angeles Times,* the *Cleveland Plain Dealer,* the *Chicago Tribune, Human Resource Executive,* and *O, the Oprah Magazine.* She is co-author of three Berrett-Koehler books: *A Peacock in the Land of Penguins (Third edition, 2001), What Would Buddha Do at Work? (2001),* and *Customer at the Crossroads (2000).* To learn more, go to www.peacockproductions.com.

Shedding Light on Winter Dreams
by Paul Levesque

Rob Walpole felt that the waterfront area in his Canadian hometown of Owen Sound (near Lake Huron's Georgian Bay) was lacking a "certain something," especially during the cold, dark winter evenings. He believed something should be done to draw people into the downtown area, to help dispel the winter doldrums.

A metal worker by trade, Rob approached the city council with an offer to build a series of displays to be installed in parkland near the river—displays decorated with festive colored lights. The city expressed little enthusiasm for the idea, but gave him permission to proceed on his own initiative.

Encouraged by his wife and his mother, Rob first built a miniature storybook train locomotive. This was followed by a half-scale model of a biplane, complete with Snoopy in the cockpit. Gratified to see how local families were attracted to the displays, Rob continued to build more.

"You'd walk along the riverbank on a blustery [wintry] day," recalls city councilor Ann Kelly, "and you'd think, 'What do I see, on the horizon?' It looked like a shape. That would be Rob, all by himself, out in the blizzard, setting up the displays." Before long, Rob's labor of love began to attract support from local businesses and volunteers, and continued to expand.

Today, Owen Sound's *Festival of Northern Lights* extends along several city blocks, and incorporates strings of lights totaling over eight miles in length. The festival attracts daily busloads of tourists from other communities in the region.

In 2002 the city formally bestowed special Dreamcrafter awards on Rob and Marie—and in the process officially made Owen Sound Canada's first Dreamcrafting Community. The city now makes annual awards to individuals who have similarly made a difference in their community.

For Rob, the real reward has been seeing the effect of his fantasyland of lights on young people. "I just get such a kick out of watching these kids," he says. "You go down there tonight, and you see these parents walk along hand in hand with their kids, they're laughing, and Dad's carrying them . . . and I know that's things they'll remember. I know that's what *I* remember. And that's just so great."

Anyone can experience the same great feeling, of course. Colored lights are not the only way to add color and light to our communities, our workplaces, our lives. Achieving *any* kind of big dream will be rewarding. It's a process that involves a number of key elements:

Aspiration—We begin by making the initial decision to do something that matters to us, igniting a sense of mission about it within ourselves.

Motivation—We must pause and celebrate key milestones along the way, to intensify and maintain our resolve over the long term.

Inclusion—We've got to get others involved, and share the glory, to make our dream feel like *their* dream too.

Even if what we choose to do seems small and trivial, these things have a way of growing. The feeling has a way of spreading.

"It's the feel-good feeling," as Marie describes it. "[The feeling] that you've done something that other people are getting so much enjoyment out of. It's been fun. It's really been fun. You're never too old to have a dream."

○

Paul Levesque is author (with Art McNeil) of *Dreamcrafting: The Art of Dreaming Big, The Science of Making It Happen (Berrett-Koehler, 2003).*

No More Homeless Pets
by Mary Hessler-Key

I thought I wasn't hearing correctly. "Did you say 31,700 cats and dogs?" I asked hesitating. "That's correct. For every 87 cats and dogs brought into the county shelter each day, 73 are euthanized. That comes to a little over 26,500 a year," replied Bill Armstrong, the head of animal control. "Wow. It's hard to believe that our community tolerates that!" I reacted.

Bill has the tough job of running animal control in our county. His facility is a place of last resort where most animals that enter never leave. The number of cats and dogs "put to sleep" each year is staggering and adoption doesn't make a dent in the numbers. While the animals that are healthy and have a good temperament are placed into adoption, the vast majority of animals coming into this county shelter will die by lethal injection and be cremated.

WORK WITH CITY HALL

In Florida where I live, we have a disproportionate number of feral cat colonies. One of the reasons for this is that the warm weather affords an extra birthing season. Feral cats are the subject of a bitter controversy here; the Florida Fish and Wildlife Conservation Commission (FWC) sees feral cats as threats to endangered birds and other wildlife, and does not support Trap/Neuter/Release programs on commission-managed lands. Worse yet, the FWC has attempted to put into law the right of its officers to destroy feral cat colonies that they deem dangerous to birds. Animal welfare groups want to spay and neuter the colonies and let them live out their lives until the colonies become extinct through aging. Programs in San Francisco and other places show that sterilized feral cat colonies have few negative impacts on the community and are a critical factor in ending the needless cycle of unwanted animals.

With a passion for making a deplorable situation better, Bill got involved in a newly forming coalition of animal welfare advocates called No More Homeless Pets (NMHP). NMHP has a simple purpose—to stop the euthanasia of healthy cats and dogs in our community. Bill attended NMHP meetings for over a year before becoming a member. As an animal control officer in the state and subject to its laws and politics, Bill made the decision to be part of NMHP despite the fact that feral cat supporters are part of this same coalition. He faced criticism from his more conservative peers who are not supportive of Trap/Neuter/Release programs or any attempts to negotiate on this emotional issue. Despite the pressure, Bill could not deny his ethics and felt there must be some solution or compromise. His joining NMHP took tremendous courage.

Bill's presence has completed a circle. Now the entire community of animal welfare agencies and advocates are united in eradicating this problem. Bill's presence allows us to apply for grants that require community-wide collaboration. The lesson I've learned from Bill is that acting on your own convictions can tip the scale one way or the other. Fortunately for NMHP, Bill went from observer to active member of our coalition. Other animal control officers would not be as brave and would fear a reprisal from state authorities. In whatever we are passionate about, it's important to get clear on our stance (even if it takes a while) and to find ways that we can support what we believe is right and reflect our commitment in all we do.

- Ask: What am I passionate about and can I make a difference?
- If my stance is controversial and could get me in trouble, think about ways that the situation could be a "win" for all involved; if it can't be, ask: Am I willing to live with what might happen?
- Take steps, even if initially small, to forward your idea or cause.

○

Mary Hessler-Key, Ph.D., is an international consultant, executive coach, and speaker. She specializes in helping entrepreneurs leave a legacy that positively impacts their business. Dr. Key is the author of two books, *The Entrepreneurial*

WORK WITH CITY HALL

Cat: 13 Ways to Transform Your Worklife (Berrett-Koehler, 1999) and *What Animals Teach Us (Random House, 2001).* For more information visit: www.marykeyassociates.com and also the No More Homeless Pets website, www.nmhp-hc.org.

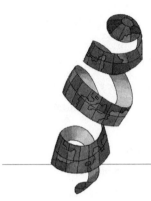

STAND UP TO
AUTHORITY

Speaking Truth to Power
by BJ Gallagher

Word spread like wildfire across campus that Monday. "Did you hear what Warren Bennis told the Board of Trustees over the weekend?" my friend Alan asked me.

Dr. Bennis, former president of the University of Cincinnati and now a distinguished business professor at the University of Southern California (USC), had been invited to speak to the board at their annual gathering in La Quinta, outside Palm Springs. Inducing such a prominent, well-published leadership expert to teach at USC was quite a coup, and the board was eager to see their prize recruit in action.

"No, what did he say?" I replied.

Alan could hardly contain his excitement as he related the tale: "He stood up and told the board that 'The problem with this university is that it's over-managed and under-led!' Can you believe it?"

I nodded and smiled. Sounds like Warren, I thought to myself. I had just met him a few months earlier, but in that meeting, who he was as a leader and a human being radiated like a powerful lighthouse beacon.

Earlier that year, I had heard Professor Bennis's name on the lips of many people—faculty, staff, and even people I met off-campus. "Warren Bennis says this" and "Warren Bennis says that" I heard again and again, as if he were the ultimate authority on Important Matters. Who is this guy, I wondered, and why is everybody quoting him all the time? I decided to find out for myself.

I called his office and invited him to lunch at the Faculty Center. He was charming and gracious when we met, but he looked more like a movie star than a distinguished professor—sparkling blue eyes set in a handsome, deeply tanned face, with gorgeous, thick white hair. After getting situated at our table, I came straight to the point. "I keep hearing people quote you all the time. So tell me, why are you famous?"

He flashed a dazzling smile, and teased, "I think you know already."

"Well, I know you were president of the University of Cincinnati, but what else?" I persisted.

He demurred again, deflecting the conversation, "I'm much more interested in your experience here at USC. How long have your worked here? What do you like about it? What kind of future do you see for the university?" His attention and curiosity were irresistible, and our wonderful conversation ranged over many topics during our midday repast.

I learned several important things from Warren that day. First, I saw the power in the way he makes people feel special, important, and valuable. When I talk with any other powerful, famous man, I always come away with the sense that he is the smartest person in the world. But when I talked with Warren, I came away feeling like *I'm* the smartest person in the world!

Second, I learned that leaders don't just *say* the right things—they *do* the right things. A true leader walks his talk, even if it means delivering bad news to the people who hired him. Warren gave the Board of Trustees his honest assessment of the problem, even though he knew it would displease them. He acted on the courage of his convictions in speaking truth to power.

Finally, and perhaps most important, I learned that when your work speaks for itself, don't interrupt. People like Warren, who are making a difference in the world, don't have a need to brag about it.

TIPS

- When was the last time you made it a point to make someone else the center of attention? How does it benefit them, and is there something in it for you, too?
- When other people watch what you do, is it apparent that you walk your talk, or are your words and deeds incongruent? How can you be sure?
- What one problem do you see in your organization that you are willing to take on, even if it means speaking truth to power?

○

BJ Gallagher is a consultant, speaker, and author, specializing in diversity, personal accountability, values and ethics, and gender issues in the workplace. Her clients include IBM, Nissan, Chevron, John Deere Credit, and DaimlerChrysler, among others. She is co-author of three Berrett-Koehler books: *A Peacock in the Land of Penguins (Third edition, 2001)*, *What Would Buddha Do at Work? (2001)*, and *Customer at the Crossroads (2000)*. To learn more, go to www.peacockproductions.com.

The Courageous Accountant
by Bill Treasurer

The early 2000s were enough to jade even the most ardent capitalist. *Oh how the mighty fall . . .* and fall they did. Executives from top tier companies like Arthur Andersen, Enron, WorldCom, HealthSouth, and Tyco, perp-walking into infamy. Even homemaking diva Martha Stewart took the shameful stroll down the crooked path.

It's simplistic, and a bit pious, to think that you and I would make different choices were we in the same position as the corporate robber barons. Faced with tempting choices, the mind has a way of rationalizing *(rational lies)* anything. It takes *transcendent courage*—courage that transcends human nature—to do the right thing when the wrong thing is so enticing.

In corporate settings, courageous moments happen so infrequently these days that when they do occur, it causes us to pause and take stock of each person's capacity for personal greatness. Such was the case during a meeting I attended (as a minutes-taker) early in my career when an unlikely hero emerged from a potentially compromising situation.

The meeting was held by the "inner sanctum" of a large service company. There were twelve executives in all, mostly vice presidents of various divisions and the president they reported to. And though not a vice president, the company finance guy, Gary, was there too.

At one point, a financial issue presented itself that, construed one way, could greatly enhance the profitability of the company. And since a considerable percentage of the compensation package of each executive was directly tied to profitability, the temptation to construe the issue in a self-serving way was great. But Gary knew that pursuing such a path would put the company in a potentially precarious legal position.

It is said that absolute power corrupts absolutely. But in executive settings, money is the great corrupter. As executives weighed in with their opinions, it was easy to see the path that the executives wanted to pursue. They started devising ways that they could slip through accounting loopholes undetected. "It's in the best interest of the company," they rationalized.

The more they convinced themselves of the rightness of their decision, the more Gary grimaced. Finally, like a crossing guard at an executive schoolyard, he stretched out his arms, put his hands straight out and pronounced, "This isn't an issue of profitability, it's an issue of integrity. And as long as I am your accountant, we won't take the legally questionable path. Period."

I was sure that Gary had just laid down on a guillotine. You could see the shock on the bosses' faces. But then, as if a hypnotic spell had been broken, the president, smiling sheepishly, said, "You're right Gary. I guess that's what we pay you for. Thanks for keeping us honest."

Gary's courage was the transcendent kind. When faced with a similar dilemma, many of us would have opted for covering our own butts and giving in to our bosses' misguided desires. But Gary made a different—and more difficult—choice, to cover his bosses' butts by insisting that they be guided by their better nature, not their human nature.

- Identify the last time you had a courageous moment. What prompted your bravery?
- What acts of courage have you witnessed? What lessons about courage did you glean from watching the courageous person in action? How might you apply these lessons in your own life?

○

Bill Treasurer loves being in the midst of people's courage. He is founder of Giant Leap Consulting, a courage-building company, and the author of *Right Risk: Ten Powerful Principles For Taking Giant Leaps With Your Life (Berrett-Koehler, 2003).* He also served as the editor of this book. To learn more about Giant Leap Consulting, go to www.giantleapconsulting.com.

PAY ATTENTION TO THE LITTLE THINGS

Balance or Bust

by Beverly Kaye and Sharon Jordan-Evans

Here's a manager who truly realized that little things mean a lot.

One plant manager we heard about gives each of the ninety members of his team $150 a year to do something (anything!) to bring balance into their lives. His only request: tell me how you've used the money. The ways in which employees spend the money underscore how individual our balance needs are. Employees report spending their money on ballroom dance lessons, a drum set, gardening tools, and instruction in Tai Chi and kickboxing. One hundred and fifty dollars per person is not a lot for him to spend, and the message he sends is crystal clear. Do you have a discretionary budget that you might spend this way?

Savvy managers view work-life balance and stress-reduction initiatives as strategic business tools, not as employee perks. Do you take wellness seriously? Have you considered that there are numerous inexpensive ways to support the necessary "breaks" that all of us need in our working lives? If employees feel a balance between work and life outside of work, you are far more likely to have employees engaged, motivated, and committed.

M.A.D
TIPS

- At the end of one of your staff meetings ask everyone to share their own "balance" secrets. (You start!) You'd be surprised at how often colleagues have great ideas for dealing with stress and pressure that others on the team never thought about. Ask everyone to listen for one new idea that they might do themselves. Report out at the next staff meeting!

○

Adapted from *Love ' Em or Lose ' Em: Getting Good People to Stay.*
Beverly Kaye and Sharon Jordan-Evans have co-authored *Love ' Em or Lose ' Em: Getting Good People to Stay (Berrett-Koehler, 1999)*, now available in 17 languages and recognized as the world's best-selling employee retention book. Their latest book, *Love It, Don't Leave It: 26 Ways to Get What You Want at Work (Berrett-Koehler, 2003)* offers "anyone who works" easy-to-implement strategies for increasing job satisfaction. Beverly is the founder and CEO of Career Systems International, and Sharon is the president of the Jordan Evans Group.

No Lizards in My Shoes
by Perry J. Ludy

While on vacation in Aruba, the villa that my wife and I were staying in was always immaculate. Dishes were washed, there was always an abundance of clean towels, and our personal laundry was always washed, dried, and folded. However we did notice one unusual thing. Everyday upon returning to the villa, our shoes, though previously lined up perfectly on the floor, were always arranged neatly on a hanging shoe rack.

After the third day, I had to ask Jane, our housekeeper, why did the resort ask her to arrange our shoes on the shoe rack? She replied, "There is no instruction or training that calls for me to rack the shoes. This is something I do because I know that if the villa is perfect, you will return. If everyone comes back, I can keep my job."

Jane then proceeded to tell me the following story: "Years ago, a female customer was dressing for a very important dinner. Carefully she pulled a pair of beautiful shoes out of the closet. As she held the shoes in her hand, a good-sized lizard quickly ran up her arm and over her shoulder. Until that point, this lady had been a regular customer at the hotel. After the lizard, she never returned. So, I rack my customers' shoes every day since. There will never be lizards in your shoes! I don't want you to have a memory like that when you think about Tierra del Sol!"

Well, it doesn't take much to see what would happen if each of us took a similar approach within our organizations, of doing one small thing to ensure that our customers return or have a pleasant memory of a product or a service we made available. These small but MAD steps would take our organizations into a period of outstanding customer service never before seen, and there would never be a lizard in our shoes.

- Pay attention to the little details. They can make a big difference. It doesn't matter how expensive your shoes are, if there's a pebble in your shoe you're going to forget all about your shiny shoes!

○

Perry Ludy has over 25 years' experience in senior-level executive positions with leading corporations and entrepreneurial companies, including PepsiCo and Procter & Gamble. He is author of the book *Profit Building: Cutting Costs Without Cutting People (Berrett-Koehler, 2000).*

Lennhart's Law: Little Things Make the Biggest Difference

by Leslie A. Yerkes

In business, little things—the things we do hundreds of times a day—count as much or more than large ones—things that happen once a year or even once a lifetime. The difference you make every day is the sum total of your "little" choices. In the long run, it's little things that make the lasting impressions and the most significant changes. Cumulatively, little things add up to create a large impact. A one-thousand-pound bomb can make a crater thirty feet across in an instant; water, one drip at a time over thousands of years, can create the Grand Canyon. In much the same way, taking care of the *little* things is one way to make a positive difference in the world.

Let me tell you a story.

I was late. I was loaded down with packages, traffic was insane, and it was threatening to rain. My hand was raised and waving in the International Hailing Signal but I couldn't get a taxi to even slow down, much less stop. So I turned and started walking back to my hotel, packages banging off my legs.

Soon, I felt the first drop of rain and decided to give it one last, half-hearted wave. I got lucky. And Stockholm Taxi No. 7 got a passenger.

I speak virtually no Swedish so I asked the driver if he spoke English.

"Not well," he said, "but enough."

PAY ATTENTION TO THE LITTLE THINGS

I asked if I could give him directions with my hands and he laughed. Then he turned to look at me, smiled, and said, "Jah!"

And so I did.

Between gestures, I asked him questions. I discovered my driver was retired from government service, was formerly in human resources, had a passion for good books, and that his name was Lennhart. I also asked Lennhart why he stopped to pick me up when no other taxi would.

"I cannot say why they did not stop for you. That is their business. But I stopped because you were getting wet and needed a ride. And that is what I do. I keep people dry and I take them places. It is not much but I try to do it well."

Not only did Lennhart keep me dry and get me where I was going, but as we traveled and talked, he became my friend. He told me tales of Stockholm and his previous employment, and how his department should have read my book *Fun Works*.

Like water forming the Grand Canyon, Lennhart's little thing of doing his job well keeps having its effect. Today when I travel to Stockholm, Lennhart is my personal chauffeur. And he is the first choice of many of my friends to whom I have given his name. His retirement business of being a cab driver is flourishing.

But Lennhart's most important job is being a teacher. Every passenger who enters his taxi learns Lennhart's Law: it's the little things that make a difference. Here are the action steps of Lennhart's Law that can make a big difference in your life, both personal and professional:

1. Be polite: shake hands, look 'em in the eye.
2. Learn someone's name and use it often.
3. Ask more questions than you give answers.

4. Respect everyone—even when they don't deserve it.

Today, I make sure that I follow Lennhart's Law every time I can. And Lennhart? Well, in his own way, the driver of Stockholm Taxi No 7 is making a difference and changing the world.

One passenger at a time.

○

Leslie Yerkes is an organizational development and change management consultant in Cleveland, OH and the owner of Catalyst Consulting Group, Inc. *Beans: Four Principles for Running a Business in Good Times or Bad (Jossey-Bass Publishers, 2003)* is Leslie's third book. Her previous books, *Fun Works (Berrett-Koehler, 2001)* and *301 Ways to Have Fun at Work (Berrett-Koehler, 1997)* continue to be leading business sellers on Amazon.com. Contact Leslie Yerkes at 216-241-3939 or at fun@catalystconsulting.net or www.changeisfun.com.

PAY ATTENTION TO THE LITTLE THINGS

EXPRESS GRATITUDE

Attracting More Acknowledgment
by Jan Stringer

"Simplicity, order, harmony, beauty, and joy—All the other principles that can transform your life will not blossom and flourish without gratitude." —Sarah Ban Breathnach, *Simple Abundance.*

While a vice president of sales for a telecommunications company, I learned the importance of expressing acknowledgment and gratitude, even when there did not seem to be anything to acknowledge.

One constant issue that confronted our team was the long sales cycle in our business. It took many phone calls, action steps, letters, appointments, proposals, and negotiation conversations to close a sale. Through that process, I could see the excitement of each salesperson diminishing as the cycle extended over several months. It was easy to feel as if we weren't achieving any results.

I am a strong proponent of the concept that we create our realities with our perceptions—to change our realities all we have to do is change our perceptions—and we change our perceptions by expressing gratitude for what we have received instead of focusing on what we are lacking. So, I decided to create an atmosphere of accomplishment by implementing a monthly meeting to share self-acknowledgments.

The first meeting began with a heavy feeling in the air. The heaviness was caused by the burden that the salespeople were carrying due to the dissatisfaction they felt with their results.

The purpose of the meeting was for each person to share about what they did and did not accomplish. Then each person was acknowledged by their fellow team members for something that was noteworthy. Most of the time, the accomplishment was NOT a sale. A typical acknowledgment might be "I would like to acknowledge how you always have a smile on your face and how you always keep the team laughing."

At the end of each meeting, the whole team, including and especially me, was much lighter and happier. Every person had the opportunity to clear the air, to restore their self-esteem, and to regain what was lost along the way during the sales process. This was worth the time and energy expended a million times over.

The ultimate benefit for the company was that people kept playing the sales game—even when they didn't produce the results they were expecting or hoping to produce. In addition, they played the sales game longer and more effectively. Most importantly, they didn't carry over the failures of the last month into the next month.

If you would like to create your own atmosphere of accomplishment and self-acknowledgment, I recommend that each person on your team:

1. Sets aside time each day for expressing gratitude for the number of perfect customers that have been served by your company, the amount of sales received, the lines of credit received, etc.
2. Throughout the day, keeps a running list of all their accomplishments—from the small to the large. Writes these accomplishments down in a journal and begins each statement with "I acknowledge myself for . . . "
3. At the end of each day, makes an accounting of how well they feel they have accomplished their mission that day. Just as we count the money we receive and expend in the course of doing business each day, it is an important discipline to bring one's self to account at the end of the day so as to know from where to start the next morning.

I invite you to stop for a moment and begin now creating an atmosphere of accomplishment and self-acknowledgment for yourself and your team.

○

Jan Stringer is central executive officer, PerfectCustomers, Inc., and co-author of *Attracting Perfect Customers (Berrett-Koehler, 2001)*. To learn more, go to: www.perfectcustomers.com.

Touchy-Feely Is Not My Style
by Cindy Ventrice

When Alan sat down in his chair in my management training course on recognition, I knew he was going to be a tough man to convince of the value of acknowledging employee contributions. The arguments he would offer were already whispering in my ear. "Why should I recognize them? They get paid to do their job." "I've been on the receiving end of recognition. I have plaques, certificates, t-shirts, and pins. They're all meaningless." "I have enough to do already. You can't expect me to add something else to my list."

But Alan was there for the day. He had to be. His company was requiring all of its managers to attend. That didn't mean that he had to like it and it didn't mean that he couldn't try to sway everyone to his way of thinking. After all, some of his employees had been with him for over ten years. If they were *that* unhappy, they would have left by now. Alan told us, "This touchy-feely stuff might work for some managers, but it is just not my style."

By the end of the day Alan wasn't arguing any longer, but did that mean that he agreed or did he just get tired? He didn't complete an evaluation. I figured I would never know for sure if the workshop or the testimonials of his fellow managers had any impact on him. I hoped that he would do things just a little differently from then on.

Fast-forward one month. I am having a conversation with a friend and the subject turns to recognition. "Oh, I have a story for you!" she says. It has come through the grapevine. One friend told another, my friend has heard it, and now she is telling me.

It seems that this woman, a secretary for a medium-sized company (one I am quite familiar with) was ecstatic about the recognition she had recently received. She had worked for the same guy for ten years. He was tough to work for, but the job was a good one. That is not what she was excited about, however. It was that after ten years, for the first time ever, her boss Alan had thanked her for the job she did. He told her that she made the department run smoothly. That without her, his job would be ten times harder.

Alan had taken a risk. He did something he had never done before. The result was that his secretary wasn't just pleased to be acknowledged, she was bubbling over with her own gratitude. Do you think he has any idea what a difference he made?

M.A.D
TIPS

- Make a list of the people who assist you on a regular basis.
- Find a way to let each person know how grateful you are.
- Make gratitude a habit. For more ideas on how to do this go to www.maketheirday.com.

○

Cindy Ventrice is the author of *Make Their Day! Employee Recognition That Works (Berrett-Koehler, 2003)*. A speaker, trainer, and consultant with over twenty years' experience, Cindy works with organizations to solve employee morale issues. You can learn more at: www.maketheirday.com.

Courageous Gratitude
by Bill Treasurer

Sometimes the best way to make an enduring difference in people's lives is to let them know you care about them. For a number of reasons, this is hardest to do in corporate settings. In a world of shifting client demands, compressed deadlines, constantly rising expectations, and cutthroat competition, saying *thank you* seems like a luxury, if not a downright weakness.

Some executives avoid expressions of gratitude because they expect people to do a good job because they're paid to. Others avoid it because they're too busy or absentminded. Still others don't express gratitude because they're so uncomfortable receiving it themselves. And more than one executive has offered the excuse, "I just wasn't brought up that way."

Knowing how hard it is to say *thank you* at work, it took me by complete surprise when David, a partner in one of the world's largest consulting firms, went "off agenda" for the sole purpose of saying thank you. I had been brought in to lead a workshop on Courageous Leadership, and had worked closely with David and his "lieutenants" to create a tight agenda.

Truthfully, I was a bit annoyed. You lose a lot of control when the client decides to fly solo, and there's no telling where he or she will take the group. More than a few leadership retreats have been ruined because of the leader's strong sense of self-importance. But sensing this moment was different, I withheld my protests. And I'm glad I did. No lesson on courageous leadership could ever have had the impact of what I saw next.

After clearing his throat, David spoke. "The reason I don't do this much is because it's hard for me to do. I don't know why, it just is. But since today is all about courage, I'm going to stretch my comfort zone. Bear with me."

Then David stood in front of each direct report, looked them in the eyes, and told them how much he appreciated them.

I'd never seen an executive get this vulnerable in front of his people before. David was out on the edge. He wasn't just stretching his comfort zone, he was outside of it altogether. In a few instances, David's voice got shaky and he had to pause and regain his composure. Nearly everyone in the room, including me, had gotten welled up with emotion, partly because what David was saying was so rawly honest and heartfelt, and partly because we were witnessing a man in the midst of his courage. David was being a courageous leader, the hard way: the way of vulnerability, the way of gratitude.

A deep silence fell over the room when he was done. David had just given each person a gift—the recognition that they were valued. Deeply and sincerely.

Making a difference, particularly in a corporate setting, takes more than grand plans. It takes more than chutzpah and audacity. And it certainly takes more than money. It takes elevating the self-worth of all the people who are working so hard to get the difference made. It doesn't cost a thing to let someone know they are valued. It just takes a hearty *thank you.*

- Identify what you're thankful for relative to each team member's contribution.
- List the ways that you could express gratitude to each person, based on how they like to be recognized.
- When all else fails, when you feel at a loss for words, and when you're worried about not seeming sincere, just say two words: *thank you.*

○

Bill Treasurer loves being in the midst of people's courage. He is founder of Giant Leap Consulting, a courage-building company, and the author of *Right Risk: Ten Powerful Principles For Taking Giant Leaps With Your Life (Berrett-Koehler, 2003).* He also served as the editor of this book. To learn more about Giant Leap Consulting, go to www.giantleapconsulting.com.

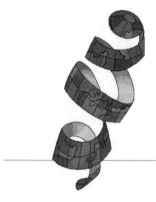

INDEX

183

INDEX

186

INDEX

INDEX

Berrett-Koehler Publishers

Berrett-Koehler is an independent publisher of books and other publications at the leading edge of new thinking and innovative practice on work, business, management, leadership, stewardship, career development, human resources, entrepreneurship, and global sustainability.

Since the company's founding in 1992, we have been committed to creating a world that works for all by publishing books that help us to integrate our values with our work and work lives, and to create more humane and effective organizations.

We have chosen to focus on the areas of work, business, and organizations, because these are central elements in many people's lives today. Furthermore, the work world is going through tumultuous changes, from the decline of job security to the rise of new structures for organizing people and work. We believe that change is needed at all levels—individual, organizational, community, and global—and our publications address each of these levels.

Right Risk
10 Powerful Principles for Taking Giant Leaps with Your Life

Bill Treasurer

In *Right Risk,* Bill Treasurer draws on the experiences and insights of successful risk-takers (including his own experiences as daredevil high diver "Captain Inferno") to detail ten principles that readers can use to take risks with greater intelligence and confidence.

Paperback, 200 pages • ISBN 1-57675-246-1
Item #52461 $15.95

Berrett-Koehler Publishers
PO Box 565, Williston, VT 05495-9900
Call toll-free! **800-929-2929** 7 am-9 pm EST
Or fax your order to 1-802-864-7626

For fastest service order online: **www.bkconnection.com**
Visit our website to find out about our new books, special offers, free excerpts, or to subscribe to our free monthly eNewsletter

Books by the contributing authors of
Positively M.A.D.

Abdullah, Sharif
*Creating a World That
Works for All*
1-57675-062-0 $15.00

Adams, Marilee
*Change Your Questions,
Change Your Life*
1-57675-241-0 $14.95

Axelrod, Dick
Terms of Engagement
1-57675-239-9 $24.95

Axelrod, Dick and Emily
*You Don't Have to
Do It Alone*
1-57675-278-X $16.95

Bell, Chip
Customers As Partners
1-881052-78-8 $17.95

*Managers As Mentors,
2nd Edition*
1-57675-142-2 $19.95

Dance Lessons
1-57675-043-4 $24.95

Magnetic Service
1-57675-236-4 $24.95

Blanchard, Ken
*Empowerment Takes More
Than a Minute, 2nd Edition*
1-57675-153-8 $14.95

Full Steam Ahead!
1-57675-153-8 $14.95

Managing By Values
1-57675-274-7 $14.95

The Secret
1-57675-289-5 $19.95

The 3 Keys to Empowerment
1-57675-160-0 $14.95

Brogniez, Jan
Attracting Perfect Customers
1-57675-124-4 $18.95

Chaleff, Ira
*The Courageous Follower,
2nd Edition*
1-57675-247-X $18.95

Coles, Carol
*The Ultimate Competitive
Advantage*
1-57675-167-8 $36.95

Cunningham, Storm
Restoration Economy
1-57675-191-0 $29.95

Derber, Charles
*Regime Change Begins at
Home*
1-57675-292-5 $19.95

Frick, Don
Robert K. Greenleaf
1-57675-276-3 $29.95

Hateley, BJ
*Peacock in the Land of
Penguins, 3rd Edition*
1-57675-173-2 $15.95

Gordon, Pamela
Lean and Green
1-57675-170-8 $24.95

Halal, William
The New Management
1-57675-032-9 $19.95

Haynes, David
The Peon Book
1-57675-285-2 $12.95

Berrett-Koehler Publishers
PO Box 565, Williston, VT 05495-9900
Call toll-free! **800-929-2929** 7 am-9 pm EST

Or fax your order to 1-802-864-7626
For fastest service order online: **www.bkconnection.com**

Hessler-Key, Mary
The Entrepreneurial Cat
1-57675-064-7 $9.95

Holman, Peggy
Change Handbook
1-57675-058-2 $49.95

Izzo, John
Second Innocence
1-57675-263-1 $14.95

Jacobs, Robert
*You Don't Have to
Do It Alone*
1-57675-278-X $16.95

Real Time Strategic Change
1-57675-030-2 $24.95

Janoff, Sandra
Future Search, 2nd Edition
1-57675-081-7 $27.95

Jordan-Evans, Sharon
*Love 'Em or Lose 'Em,
2nd Edition*
1-57675-140-6 $20.95

Love It, Don't Leave It
1-57675-250-X $17.95

Katz, Judith
Inclusion Breakthrough
1-57675-139-2 $26.95

Kaye, Beverly
*Love 'Em or Lose 'Em,
2nd Edition*
1-57675-140-6 $20.95

Love It, Don't Leave It
1-57675-250-X $17.95

Kennedy, Debbe
*Diversity Breakthrough!
Strategic Action Series*
1-58376-025-3 $58.95

Leider, Richard
The Power of Purpose
1-57675-021-3 $20.00

*Claiming Your Place
at the Fire*
1-57675-297-6 $14.95

*Repacking Your Bags,
2nd Edition*
1-57675-180-5 $16.95

Whistle While You Work
1-57675-103-1 $16.95

Working Naturally
1-58376-072-5 $8.95

Levesque, Paul
Dreamcrafting
1-57675-229-1 $15.95

Levine, Stewart
The Book of Agreement
1-57675-179-1 $17.95

Getting to Resolution
1-57675-115-5 $17.95

Levy, Mark
Accidental Genius
1-57675-083-3 $15.95

Ludy, Perry
Profit Building
1-57675-108-2 $27.95

Manz, Charles
*The Leadership Wisdom
of Jesus*
1-57675-066-3 $15.95

Emotional Discipline
1-57675-230-5 $15.95

The Power of Failure
1-57675-132-5 $14.95

*The Wisdom of Soloman
at Work*
1-57675-085-X $20.00

Marx, Robert
*The Wisdom of Soloman
at Work*
1-57675-085-X $20.00

Mitchell, Donald
*The Ultimate Competitive
Advantage*
1-57675-167-8 $36.95

Oshry, Barry
Leading Systems
1-57675-072-8 $24.95

Seeing Systems
1-881052-99-0 $24.95

Pattakos, Alex
Prisoners of Our Thoughts
1-57675-288-7 $22.95

Perkins, John
*Confessions of an
Economic Hit Man*
1-57675-301-8 $24.95

Raelin, Joe
*Creating Leaderful
Organizations*
1-57675-233-X $22.95

Reina, Michelle
*Trust and Betrayal in
the Workplace*
1-57675-070-1 $27.95

Shea, Heather
Dance Lessons
1-57675-043-4 $24.95

Online Learning Today
1-57675-143-0 $18.95

Schmaltz, David
*The Blind Men and the
Elephant*
1-57675-253-4 $18.95

Shapiro, David
*Choosing the Right Thing
to Do*
1-57675-057-4 $15.95

*Claiming Your Place
at the Fire*
1-57675-297-6 $14.95

*Repacking Your Bags,
2nd Edition*
1-57675-180-5 $16.95

Whistle While You Work
1-57675-103-1 $16.95

Stahl-Wert, John
The Serving Leader
1-57675-308-5 $14.95

Stoner, Jesse
Full Steam Ahead!
1-57675-306-9 $14.95

Ventrice, Cindy
Make Their Day!
1-57675-197-X $18.95

Walters, Jamie
Big Vision, Small Business
1-57675-188-0 $17.95

Weisbord, Marvin
*Discovering Common
Ground*
1-881052-08-7 $28.95

Future Search, 2nd Edition
1-57675-081-7 $27.95

Yerkes, Leslie
Fun Works
1-57675-154-6 $18.95

*301 Ways to Have Fun
at Work*
1-57675-019-1 $16.95